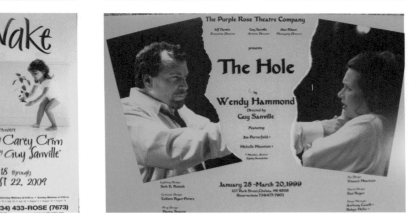

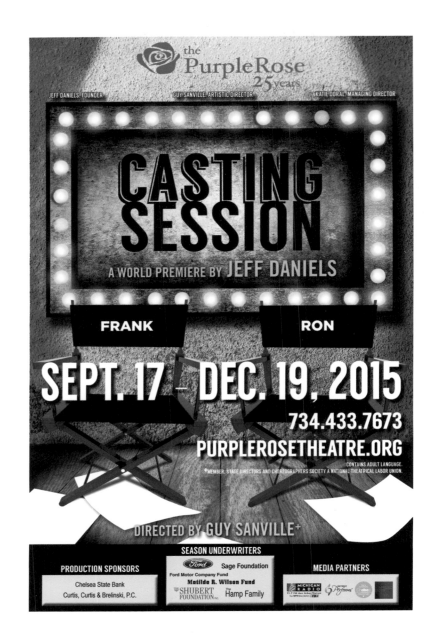

The
Purple Rose
of CHELSEA

25 Years *of Passion, Principles, and Performances*

CYNTHIA FURLONG REYNOLDS

Written by Cynthia Furlong Reynolds
www.CynthiaFurlongReynolds.org

Design and layout by Marty Somberg / Somberg Design
www.sombergdesigns.com

Printed by University Lithoprinters, Inc. / Ann Arbor, Michigan

10 9 8 7 6 5 4 3 2 1
Library of Congress Cataloging-in-Publication Data on file
ISBN: 978-0-9855923-5-6

Acknowledgements: Sincere thanks to Katie Doral and Gerie Greenspan for hiring me;
Katie for editing long into the night; Guy Sanville and Michelle Mountain for allowing
me to tail them for months on end, sharing their wisdom and insight; Danna Segrest for
a magnificent job reviewing photographs; Julia Garlotte, Julia Cassell, Richard Ferguson-
Wagstaffe for behind-the-scenes work; and, of course, Jeff Daniels, for providing such
a fabulous story!

CONTENTS

All the world's a stage,

And all the men and women merely players;

They have their exits and their entrances,

And one man in his time plays many parts.

—WILLIAM SHAKESPEARE, *AS YOU LIKE IT*

CHAPTER 1

THE FOUNDER
Jeff Daniels

Jeff Daniels starred in Chelsea High School and Chelsea Area Players productions.

Actor. Playwright. Director. Singer. Songwriter. Guitarist. Band member. Founding father of the acclaimed Purple Rose Theatre. Star of stage and screens, both large and small. At the age of sixty, Jeff Daniels stars in an extremely long résumé.

"I'm a very creative person—Jim Carey told me I was kind of like a shark in water—sharks are compelled to keep swimming. Constantly," he says, grinning. He leans back in his desk chair, puts his hands behind his head and his bare feet on his desk as he begins the story of his career and the origins of the theater that bears his creative imprint.

His acting career began early—in the sixth grade—when DiAnn L'Roy, his music teacher, asked him to do an improvisational skit. He played a politician delivering a speech while struggling to keep his pants from falling down. The boy had his audience in such an uproar that other teachers and students ran into the room to see what was so funny. The louder they laughed, the funnier the skit became. "I knew then what I wanted to do with the rest of my life," he says, crediting L'Roy with introducing him to his life-long passion.

During his high school years, between sports schedules and work schedules at his father's business, the Chelsea Lumber Company, the boy auditioned for school and community theater productions. When he enrolled at Central Michigan University, he decided to test his theatrical skills against other student performers. During his third year at CMU, he was sitting in the library reading *Central Michigan Life* ("Instead of doing my homework," he points out) when he saw an announcement about auditions to be held at Eastern Michigan University for a four-play spring repertory festival. Once again, he decided to see how he "stacked up" against other aspiring young actors.

The twenty-one-year-old packed up and headed to New York City, a brand new guitar in hand.

Jeff and Kathleen Daniels on their wedding day.

He appeared at the auditions dressed in jeans and a sweatshirt, with Red Wings tickets in his pocket. Most of the others auditioning were, he recalls, "dressed for dinner, spiffed up, practicing monologues from Shakespeare." Daniels had prepared a piece from Henry Ibsen's *The Caretaker*, playing a quiet mentally ill brother. As he waited for his turn through a very long day, he repeatedly checked the time. "When I finished my monologue, I thought I'd done pretty well. I waited to see if I was called back, but I kept looking at the clock, calculating how long I had before I had to leave for the game."

When callbacks were finally posted, Jeff Daniels' name was on the list. So was Rory Murphy's, a classmate at CMU. By dinnertime, they were waiting for the next round of callbacks, and Jeff Daniels was debating whether or not to leave. But Rory grabbed his arm and told him, "I'm gonna tell you something you'll thank me for. The AD [Artistic Director] of the Circle Rep[ertory Theatre] knows Jim Gussett, the head of the theater department at EMU. His name is Marshall W. Mason, and he's doing this as a favor for Gussett. You're not leaving."

"So," Daniels says, "I stayed."

And his life as a performer began.

At eight o'clock that night, he was asked to read a scene from Tennessee Williams' *Summer and Smoke*. He sat facing actress Debbie Mueller while forty other aspiring actors watched. At the end of the reading, Marshall Mason announced that Daniels would have the lead in *Summer and Smoke* and appear in playwright Lanford Wilson's *Hot L Baltimore*. Daniels was stunned.

That summer he found himself challenged in an entirely new way. "Suddenly I was thrown into New York-style acting, where the directors are taking our emotions and directing us in a way that resembled public therapy, telling us, 'You've gotta go there emotionally.'" Daniels listened and learned. And impressed the renowned artistic director from New York. Before the first performance of *Summer and Smoke*, Marshall Mason pulled Daniels aside and said, "You know what you should do with your life, don't you?" He urged the college student to move to New York in the fall and join the Circle Repertory Company Marshall had co-founded—but he warned Daniels that he would have to earn his way onto the stage.

Daniels describes sitting down with his parents and telling them what Mason had told him. His mother suggested waiting until he graduated from college. His father said, "You should go."

Daniels looks out the window of his study and murmurs, "I'll never forget that moment."

The twenty-one-year-old packed up and headed to New York City, a brand new guitar in hand. "I knew I was going to a huge city where this country boy knew no one, so I bought the guitar, regarding it as a kind of friend. I'd never played a guitar in my life."

Daniels was joining an acclaimed repertory company, one *The New York Times* had called "the chief provider of new American plays." Founded in 1969 by directors Marshall Mason and Rob Thirkield, playwright Lanford Wilson, and actress Tanya Berezin, the Circle Repertory Company aimed to establish a pool of resident actors, directors, playwrights, and designers to create new plays as a team and stage them at the Sheridan Square Playhouse on Seventh Avenue. Lanford Wilson, who would win a Pulitzer Prize in Drama for *Talley's Folly* in 1980, became Daniels' mentor. Years later, many of his plays (among them *Hot L Baltimore*, *Book of Days*, *Rain Dance*, *Talley's Folly*, and *Redwood Curtain*) would be performed at the Purple Rose.

Jeff Daniels is one of a long list of distinguished actors affiliated with the Circle Repertory Company who became legendary: Alec Baldwin, Olympia Dukakis, Laurence Fishburne, Ed Harris, William Hurt, Christopher Reeve, Melissa Joan Hart, Timothy Hutton, Jennifer Jason Leigh, John Malkovich, Demi Moore, Mary-Louise Parker, Gary Sinise, Judd Hirsch, Kathy Bates, Swoosie Kurtz, Timothy Busfield, Conchatta Ferrell, Cynthia Nixon, Patricia Wettig, and Jeff Daniels.

Daniels earned his first dramatic role on stage after months of the apprenticeship when Marshall Mason cast him in Davie Storey's play *The Farm* as a last-minute replacement for Richard Gere, who had been cast in the movie *Days of Heaven*.

"In New York, when you're on stage, you're in an electric chair," Daniels says. "My early reviews were horrible. I was bad. All my confidence was gone. I was scared. I remember calling my parents and asking if I should come home. 'Stay if you can,' my mother said. I stayed."

He apprenticed for two years, living in a one-room apartment, teaching himself the guitar, and writing songs during breaks in the action. Thanks to work in a dozen commercials, he managed to support himself until he became an equity actor in 1976. A year earlier, he had seen Al Pacino in *Dog Day Afternoon*, which he considers a career turning point. "That movie convinced me that theater could be the means to an end—and I wanted that end to be movies," Daniels says. But the theater also introduced him to another passion: playwriting—"which was the fuel for my starting the Purple Rose Theatre," he says.

In 1981, Daniels made his film debut in *Ragtime*. Two years later, he played Debra Winger's husband Flap Horton in the Oscar-winning *Terms of Endearment*, which film historians consider Daniels' breakthrough role. Then came a banner year: in 1985, he appeared in *Marie* and *The Purple Rose of Cairo*. His role as Tom Baxter and Gil Shepherd in Woody Allen's *Purple Rose* earned him both a Golden Globe nomination for Best Actor in a Motion Picture Musical or Comedy and the name for a future theater. Working with Allen, he says, changed his life and career trajectory.

"I was thirty years old when *The Purple Rose of Cairo* came along. It was my step up. I knew it. And I was terrified. I asked myself, 'Am I good enough to be here?'" His question was answered when Jeffrey Kurland, Woody Allen's long-time costume designer, told Daniels, "Woody wants me to tell you that you're really good."

Daniels pauses. "I'll never forget that. I couldn't wait to rush home to our apartment and tell Kathleen. My first thought was not, 'I'm gonna be a big star,' but, 'Okay, I can make a living in the business.'"

"In New York, when you're on stage, you're in an electric chair."

Following another Golden Globe Best Actor nomination for his 1986 performance in *Something Wild*, Jeff, Kathleen, and Ben Daniels returned to their Chelsea roots.

"We operated on a shoestring budget. We begged, borrowed, adapted, and made do."

After ten years in New York City, marriage to Kathleen Treado, and the birth of their son Ben, Daniels was confronted by a friend who asked, "Why don't you go home? You've had a foot in Michigan for the last ten years. You're not committed to New York." Daniels talked the idea over with Kathleen, then checked with his agents, who told him they wouldn't object—"If you act as though you're still living down the street from our office. Just don't tell us you can't make a meeting."

Following another Golden Globe Best Actor nomination for his 1986 performance in *Something Wild*, Jeff, Kathleen, and Ben Daniels returned to their Chelsea roots. Lucas was born in 1987, followed by Nellie in 1990. "There's no question about it: that decision to move to Chelsea affected my career," Jeff Daniels conceded. "But both Kathleen and I have family here and a strong support system. We wanted to raise our kids here, and they have always come first."

Daniels began commuting long distances for projects, but by 1989, he says, he felt "creatively bored." He and Kathleen began discussing the possibility of starting a local theater company modeled after the Circle Repertory Company. "We wanted to give Michigan's twenty-one-year-olds the same opportunities I had been given," Daniels says. "We wanted to grow local talent, offering actors work on plays written by Michigan playwrights and performed on sets built by Michigan people."

While scouting locations in downtown Chelsea—which was suffering from economic doldrums and had numerous possibilities—Daniels walked into the dilapidated building next to a parking lot on Park Street and immediately realized he had found what he was looking for. The former livery stable/car dealer/bus garage/pizza shop had once been used by Daniels' grandfather, Buick dealer W.R. Daniels, to store cars, so it had a ready-made connection with the Daniels family.

"This crazy idea didn't make any business sense whatsoever, but I wouldn't do it anywhere else. We launched this theater on blind faith," Daniels says. "I thought I had enough fame to get audiences to come once. Then we'd get 'em with the quality of what we were doing."

"The Founding Four": Bart Bauer
(left) checks blueprints for the
initial theater renovations with
Jeff Daniels, Doug Beaumont, and
Artistic Director T. Newell Kring.

THE FOUNDER

Jeff Daniels bought the structure for $150,000 and undertook major renovations with the help of friends Bart Bauer and Doug Beaumont, as well as other volunteers. The first Purple Rose Theatre Board of Directors meeting convened on the construction site, around a door plopped on two sawhorses to form a makeshift table. It was a family affair. Kathleen's mother, Daphne Hodder, volunteered to take notes. His brother-in-law, Chelsea State Bank President John Mann, agreed to become treasurer. Bill Holmes of the Chelsea Milling Company soon joined them.

"We were flying by the seat of our pants." Daniels grins when he describes the early days. "The building was a tinderbox of kindling. We had a lot of demolition to do before we could start reconstruction." Maintaining a strict shoestring budget, he and his newly formed board of directors decided their first priority must be comfortable seats—purple seats—so customers would enjoy their theater experience. Everything else would be borrowed, adapted, or purchased inexpensively. Administrative offices were shoehorned into the basement and equipped with cast-off furnishings.

"We wanted people to write about life here in Michigan, about people and places familiar to our audiences."

After eight years in operation, the garage was torn down and reconstructed over sixteen months.

Once the reconstruction team was making headway, the theater ran an ad in the *Ann Arbor News* announcing open auditions to be held at the Chelsea Methodist Church, across from the construction site. Daniels hoped to identify a handful of playwrights and directors, as well as thirty actors—fifteen women and fifteen men—"who wouldn't need a lot: just molding, changing, and slapping the bad out of them."

Each actor was asked to perform two two-minute monologues, one comedic, one dramatic. "The pros nailed them," he says. "Our criteria was believability. Good actors play real people. They must absolutely believe and mean what they're saying. I learned at the Circle Rep and by doing movies—especially with Woody Allen—that an actor has to really listen and react to what the others on stage are doing. Too often we see actors pretending, not reacting. Show-and-tell acting wasn't what we wanted."

Although he quickly identified talented actors, for the first few years he could find only one director who shared his vision. And no playwrights. "We wanted people to write about life here in Michigan, about people and places familiar to our audiences," he says.

Blush at Nothing, written by Lisa Wing, launched the Purple Rose's history, performed in a theater that still smelled of sawn lumber and fresh paint. It took ten years to develop a stable of playwrights, Daniels says, so he stepped into the breach to provide the second play of the 1991 season. Set in a small town, his comedy *Shoe Man* shows how a game of golf can lead to infidelity and hilarity, as well as lessons in hitting a seven iron. Critics were enthusiastic. The *Lansing State Journal* called it "a woozie jitterbug that punishes infidelity with a seven iron to the beanie," while the *Detroit News* reported that Daniels "has a freshly wry sense of what is humorous in American culture and romance."

"I wrote *Shoe Man* thinking that if nothing else, the audience would come to see a movie star's play," Daniels says. The comedy accomplished more than just attracting growing audiences and glowing reviews; it won the first of many awards. Although Circle Rep had performed only dramas, the success of *Shoe Man* convinced Daniels that "funny sells tickets, and we wanted to introduce a growing audience to the Rose." Writing *The Tropical Pickle* in May 1992, he challenged himself to see how much humor he could pack into a play. He worked fast: opening night was Labor Day.

"We needed $300,000 to keep the doors open, so *Tropical Pickle* had a lot riding on its success—or failure," he recalls. "Fortunately, it became a hit and we played to full audiences every night. The Rose had a very encouraging start. We came out of *Tropical Pickle* with $100,000 in the bank." The play was also significant because it introduced Guy Sanville to the theater and the theater to Guy Sanville; three years later he would be named artistic director.

In the middle of the *The Tropical Pickle* run, Director Ronald Maxwell visited Chelsea to discuss casting Daniels as Colonel Joshua Chamberlain in a Civil War epic film. "I made him watch *The Tropical Pickle*," Daniels recalls. "Afterwards we went to Cleary's Pub. Out of the gate, he asked, 'Do you have the steel to play this character?' I promised I did." Based on Michael Shaara's novel *The Killer Angels*, *Gettysburg* was released in 1993, with Daniels in a starring role that became a sensation among Civil War enthusiasts. Following public clamor, the prequel *Gods and Generals* was filmed—nine years later.

In the theater's second year, Daniels established its apprenticeship program, based on the Circle Rep model. "This program was intended to give back to others, to teach twenty-one-year-old kids what they need to know about this business. It's not easy work." Now under the direction of Guy Sanville and Resident Artist Michelle Mountain, apprentices receive formal instruction as well as experience in all aspects of theater—onstage and behind the scenes. "At the end of the apprenticeship, they'll know what they need to do to become an actor, director, stage manager, or set designer in New York," Daniels says. "We emphasize reliability, professionalism, responsibility, and teamwork."

As the Purple Rose took root, Jeff Daniels perfected his skills as an expert multi-tasker. "My Dad was great at it—watching him was like watching the guy spinning plates on the *Ed Sullivan Show*," he says. "I am my father's son. Mentally I had the drive and ambition to do everything here, but physically I knew I couldn't plan to act or direct when my movie career was still on the upswing. Movies took precedence; everything else stopped for them. But I learned I could write music and plays anywhere, and when I was in town I could raise money for the Purple Rose."

Since *Shoe Man* and *The Tropical Pickle*, Daniels has written fourteen additional plays, all staging their world premieres in Chelsea: *The Vast Difference, Thy Kingdom's Coming, Escanaba in da Moonlight* (which became a motion picture), *Apartment 3A, Boom Town, Across the Way* (2002 American Theatre Critics Association Best New Play Finalist), *Norma and Wanda, Guest Artist* (2006 ATCA Best New Play Runner-Up), *Escanaba In Love, Panhandle Slim and The Oklahoma Kid, Escanaba, Best of Friends, The Meaning of Almost Everything* (2013 ATCA Best New Play Nominee), and *Casting Session*. His comedy *Casting Session* launched the theater's 25th season in September 2015.

"I find that the process of writing is such a mess. I'm swimming in words that appear to have no discipline," Daniels says. "I love to explore funky ideas and let the characters talk to me. I'm a more disciplined and a better editor now, thanks to working with Guy."

Gettysburg starred Jeff Daniels as Colonel Joshua Chamberlain, hero of Little Round Top.

"You have to connect with the crowd. You have to keep them engaged so they don't feel like, 'Man, that was two hours I'll never get back!'"

"Music was this wonderful place I could visit between movies and worries."

He also writes songs, beginning during his early days in New York. "When I was preparing to go out there, I had the feeling I'd be alone a lot, so I made the decision to take $400 I'd saved and buy a guitar. When I first arrived, Marshall let me stay at his apartment for two weeks and I was constantly writing songs—bad, bad, bad songs," he says with a grin. "The guitar has given me sanity in between phone calls—and several years ago, I could go months at a time between jobs."

The music has "kept me sane," he emphasizes, "not only during my early career, but also during a dry spell in 2008 and 2009. I could control the music. I was the editor. I was the director. I was the actor. I was everything," he says. "That's not the case as an actor. We constantly worry that we're never going to work again. That's the dark hole every actor falls into. We finish a movie and don't know what's next. It could be a phone call next week or six months from now. Or never. So music was this wonderful place I could visit between movies and worries."

Lanford Wilson nudged him into his musical career in 1978, when he suggested Daniels write music for the poem "Road Signs." Years later, when Wilson came for the first Purple

THE PURPLE ROSE *of* CHELSEA

Rose Theatre opening night, he asked Daniels' friends at Cleary's Pub afterwards if Jeff had ever played "Road Signs" for them.

"Jeff doesn't play the guitar," one friend said.

"You have to share this with people," Lanford whispered to his protégé. Jeff Daniels picked up a guitar in public for the first time that night. Soon afterwards, members of the theater board asked him if he'd consider playing the guitar as part of a fundraiser for the Purple Rose. "It was 2002, and I was so tired of raising money the conventional way," he recalls. "So I agreed. Then I discovered that was the scariest thing I'd ever done."

Between September and the Christmas holidays, he practiced daily, with mounting panic. "There was no character for me to play—actors hide behind the filter of the character," he says. "When I walked onto the stage with my guitar, I felt naked, with 110 people staring at me." It wasn't until the third year of "Jeff Daniels Onstage & Unplugged" that he discovered how to eliminate panic: create a character to hide behind. "I told myself, 'The character is Jeff Daniels in a good mood.' It worked." Since then, he has produced six albums, whose proceeds benefit the PRTC, and recently he began touring with his son Ben's band.

The opportunities offered, and the lessons learned, from his Circle Rep days stick with him in all aspects of his professional life, he says: "You have to connect with the crowd. You have to keep them engaged so they don't feel like, 'Man, that was two hours I'll never get back!'"

He not only keeps audiences engaged, he keeps reviewers happy. Daniels has received numerous awards, nominations, and honors, among them the Emmy for Outstanding Lead Actor in a Drama Series for his role as Will McAvoy in Aaron Sorkin's HBO television series *The Newsroom*; a Tony Best Actor Award nomination for the Broadway production of *God of Carnage*; and four Golden Globe Award nominations, including Best Performance by an Actor in a Motion Picture-Comedy/Musical for Woody Allen's *The Purple Rose of Cairo*.

His roles have ranged from Civil War hero Joshua Chamberlain to an unassuming dog lover in *101 Dalmatians*, a quirky single father in *Fly Away Home*, a self-consumed professor in *The Squid and the Whale*, a minister in *Because of Winn Dixie*, George Washington, the villain Zartog in the animated film *Space Chimps*, a redneck cowboy in *RV*, a professor in the indie *Howl*, the Blue Man in Mitch Albom's *The Five People You Meet in Heaven*, and Harry Dunne in *Dumb and Dumber*. He believes four films and one play define his work: *Gettysburg*, *Dumb and Dumber*, *The Squid and the Whale*, *Fly Away Home*, and *Johnny Got His Gun*, a Circle Rep performance in which "all the action takes place inside a man's mind," Daniels says. "I sat in a cage and acted out a script that consisted of ninety pages' worth of this guy's thoughts. The *New York Times* reviewer wrote, 'It does not engage our emotions,' and it closed after three weeks." He adds, "But it won an Obie because the *Village Voice* saw it and liked it."

During the theater's 25th year, Jeff Daniels has two movies slated for release (*Steve Jobs* and Ridley Scott's *The Martian*), a role on Broadway in *Blackbird*, and a part in *Allegiant I* and *II* of the *Divergent* series. He has an itinerary of band gigs with his son Ben. And he

In The Crossing, *Jeff Daniels stars as George Washington during the darkest days of the Revolution. The 2000 film won a Peabody Award for excellence.*

saw his sixteenth play, *Casting Session,* launch the anniversary season for the theater he founded. "Twenty years ago I never would have guessed that my career would be at this stage when I turned sixty," he says. "I'm very, very grateful."

Throughout his career, Daniels has followed Marshall Mason's advice the way explorers follow the North Star: *You know what you should do with your life.* "And it helps if you pick up people along the way who believe in you," he adds. "I was lucky enough to have DiAnn L'Roy, Jim Brooks (*Terms of Endearment* director), Marshall Mason, Lanford Wilson, Woody Allen, Paul Martinez (my manager), my parents, and my wife in my circle. When the journey gets rough and these people say, 'Stay,' you listen to them.

"In turn, you pass it on," he says. "That has become part of the mission of the Purple Rose. We gather talented people we enjoy working with, people who can act, direct, manage, teach, support, encourage, and correct. Together, we create art."

What new challenge could possibly remain on his horizon?

"Kathleen thinks I'll take up tap dancing next," he says with a grin. ■

"This crazy idea didn't make any business sense whatsoever... We launched this theater on blind faith. We wanted to grow local talent, offering Michigan actors work on plays written by Michigan playwrights and performed on sets built by Michigan people."

In "Jeff Daniels Onstage & Unplugged," *the actor performed with his son Ben and future daughter-in-law, Amanda Merte.*

"Twenty years ago I never would have guessed that my career would be at this stage when I turned sixty. I'm very, very grateful." —JEFF DANIELS

The old Garage Theatre, opened in 1991, was demolished eight years later, and the Purple Rose Theatre Company relocated for sixteen months. The Purple Rose Theatre opened January 11, 2001, for the first performance of Lanford Wilson's Rain Dance. Viewers filled the new 168-seat theater.

"It was a very proud day for us all," Judy Gallagher says. "That ushered in a whole new level of performances." The expansion "raised the stakes here," Guy Sanville agrees. "We got forty percent bigger, so we needed to sell forty percent more tickets to forty percent more people…Every decision had more weight."

2AZ 2015

The Vast Difference 2013

THE PURPLE ROSE *of* CHELSEA

Ties That Bind 1992

Escanaba in Da Moonlight 2011

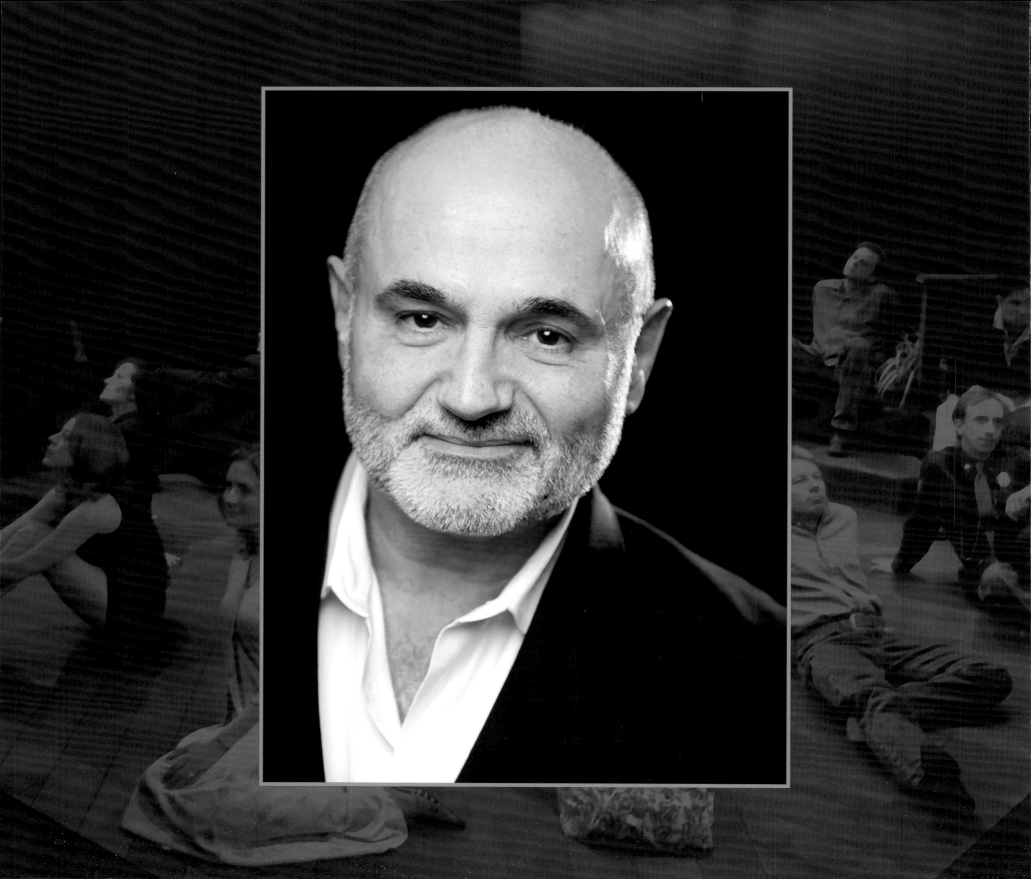

> *"Playwrights want to work with somebody who knows how to lift their work to a higher level. We give directors our blueprint, and if we give them a good blueprint, good directors will probably build something pretty close to what the playwrights intended—but much better."* — JEFF DANIELS

"**W**hat do you think a director does?" Guy Sanville asks seven apprentices early on a Friday morning at the start of their first directing workshop. "Fill in the blank:

A *director…*

"Studies a script and guides actors to do their best."

"Helps actors find the truth within the story."

"Listens first, gives impulses second."

"Offers actors directions that stimulate thought before movement."

"Creates a world where actors tell a story with meaning."

Dressed in his trademark Hawaiian shirt, shorts, sandals, and a baseball cap worn backwards, Sanville nods. "A director does everything you just said, but ultimately a director's responsibility is to exploit an actor's humanity for the understanding and entertainment of the audience. Directors find out what people—actors and audiences—know, and then they lead them to learn more."

But that's not all, he adds. "Directors also make a million decisions, from the choice of the play to the color of the door on the set. We all—stage managers, actors, set designers, lighting designers, sound experts, and the director—work together, but at the end of the day, someone has to make the call, and that person is usually the director or producer. I know how stages are built and dresses are constructed. I know how to make an actress look fifteen years older and forty pounds heavier. I know how lighting creates moods. I know how sounds and music help tell a story. I know how stories develop and how playwrights build dramatic tension. A director then has to weave all those parts together to form a picture of a place and time and the people who occupy them."

And then, he says, "The acting begins."

The Director

"The minute I walked through the doors of the Purple Rose Theatre for the first time and saw those black-and-white tiles in the lobby, I knew that this is where I belonged. I had what alcoholics call a Moment of Clarity," Guy Sanville says, plopping onto a chair in his office, which is bursting with piles of scripts, props, photos, books, costumes, awards, and mementoes. "I knew my life had changed forever."

The year? 1992. The occasion? His audition for Jeff Daniels' second play, *The Tropical Pickle*, which would conclude the theater's first full season.

Jeff Daniels enjoys telling the rest of the story. "Guy's audition was wild. It was crazy." Daniels grins as he describes the astonished reaction of the first Purple Rose Artistic Director, T. Newell Kring. "Newell watched in shock and silence as Guy performed, and he watched in shock and silence as Guy left the room. Then he wiped his brow and said, "Well, that's a no. He's nuts."

"That was crazy!" Daniels agreed. "He's perfect. I'll rewrite the part for him."

And so, with several swipes at a keyboard, a fifty-five-year-old Polish man became a thirty-six-year-old Italian, and thirty-six-year-old Guy Sanville, a native of Michigan's Upper Peninsula, found his creative home.

Born in 1953, in Escanaba—a town that Jeff Daniels would immortalize in three plays and a movie—Sanville became an actor quite accidentally. When he was a junior at Everett High School, he quit the baseball team after a dispute with the coach. As he was walking past the school auditorium, he glimpsed a beautiful young woman on stage. He stopped to see what was happening, and someone asked if he had come to read for a part. Since he had time on his hands and love on his mind, he said he was. To his surprise, he landed the lead role in the French farce *Boeing-Boeing*, and his interest in theater soared with jet propulsion.

At the age of twenty-two, he made his way to the Lansing Riverwalk Theatre, where he performed in *Bus Stop*. His first "real" director, a Michigan State professor named Marty Schulman, pulled him aside after one performance and told him, "If you stop screwing around, you could be good at this."

Those words gave the on-again, off-again college student momentum. "Jeff and I are the only people associated with the Purple Rose who don't have college degrees," he says. "I couldn't wait to get on with my career." As he auditioned for theatrical roles, he landed a variety of roles in the real world—everything from managing a paint store to delivering furniture, washing dishes, and selling shoes. "I quit jobs in order to perform in plays that paid no

Although he has earned acclaim for his acting, Sanville's longest-running role has been as Artistic Director of the Purple Rose.

Wayne David Parker and Guy Sanville appeared together in Jeff Daniels' play The Tropical Pickle (1992).

money," he says. "But every job helped prepare me for this work—and I'm still learning. My professional survival depends on that."

In 1978, at the age of twenty-four, he produced his first show—*Improvisation*—which had first appeared at the Paul Sills Story Theatre on Broadway. He advertised, auditioned, and hired the actors for the work, which was an amalgam of Grimm's fairy tales, Aesop's fables, and an anti-war theme. He also sold the advertising needed to fund the show. The following year, he took advantage of the Comprehensive Training and Employment Act (CETA), a federal jobs incentive program, and landed a theatrical position performing in children's shows in the mornings, rehearsing in the afternoons, and performing Shakespeare at night. "I learned all kinds of cool stuff during that time," he says.

In 1981, he decided to take a leap of faith to pursue his dream. He headed to New York City. An art gallery cast him in *A Doll's House*, along with Richard Thomas of *The Waltons* fame and a girl who had briefly dated a young actor named Jeff Daniels.

"I was in New York for six years, but sooner or later everyone wakes up," Sanville says, shaking his head. "I finally realized I was not going to be a movie star, but I could definitely live a creative life." He moved back to Michigan, took a job as a "repo man", married his wife Nancee, and formed the Greater Lansing Theater Lab. "In those years, to make ends meet, I worked in billing and collections at a hospital. It was a horrible job." He shudders at the memory.

When Sanville learned about *The Tropical Pickle* auditions at Jeff Daniels' new theater in Chelsea, it was almost too late for auditions. He called and landed the last audition slot. That was on a Saturday. Two days later, he was lounging in the bathtub reading *Grips, Gaffers and Best Boys: Jobs in the Film Industry* when the Purple Rose called him back for another audition. He vividly remembers memorizing his lines and arriving to find Jeff Daniels sitting next to actor Wayne David Parker, known in theater circles as Daba. "It was a scene where I'm supposed to be upset with Daba," he recalls. "I picked him up and held him. I put my all into it. Afterwards, Jeff told me he was changing the role from a fifty-two-year-old Polish guy to an Italian guy my age."

A scene from Lanford Wilson's play Book of Days (1998).

Sanville says he's "eternally grateful" for the opportunities that followed. "Years before, I swore that if I ever found a creative home, I'd stay. I found it. I've stayed."

Following his role in *The Tropical Pickle*, he was cast in Daniels' play *The Vast Difference*. Although he has earned acclaim for his acting, Sanville's longest-running role has been Artistic Director of the Purple Rose Theatre Company. In 1995, T. Newell Kring exited stage left and Jeff Daniels began searching for his replacement. One day he called Sanville for a meeting and surprised him when he said, "I've been thinking about this for a couple of weeks. I could do a national search, but I think you're the guy."

"I was stunned. Incredulous," Sanville recalls. "He believed in me! Jeff has been one of my greatest mentors and teachers. He's made me a better man. He taught me that you pick up people who believe in you and you listen to them." He adds that the fictional character he most relates to is Forrest Gump, a man who stayed true to himself, worked hard, and made the most of every opportunity that came his way.

Since that meeting in 1995, Sanville has directed more than fifty plays at the Purple Rose, including more than two dozen world premieres, among them two of Lanford Wilson's plays— *Rain Dance* and *Book of Days*—as well as fourteen of Daniels' works. Sanville has developed a unique routine for selecting plays. Once Literary Manager Michelle Mountain identifies possibilities, Sanville sits in a hot bath and reads them. If he's interested, he arranges for a reading by outstanding actors. "A play needs to be heard for it to be evaluated properly," he explains. "Here at the Rose, we like plays that use humor as a window into the human heart. A man and a woman and a problem are things I understand, things we all understand."

Over the years, the director has also considered and selected classic American plays—"but only if I have something original to say. We don't do karaoke," he qualifies. "Jeff Daniels outlined the goal for the performances we stage: to offer plays that will have special meaning to our particular audience—not necessarily to audiences in New York or L.A." Perhaps because Daniels has mastered the art of writing comedies, the Purple Rose tends to choose renowned

Sanville calls the "Escanaba" series one of his career milestones. Here he works with former apprentices Jake Christensen and Charlyn Swarthout.

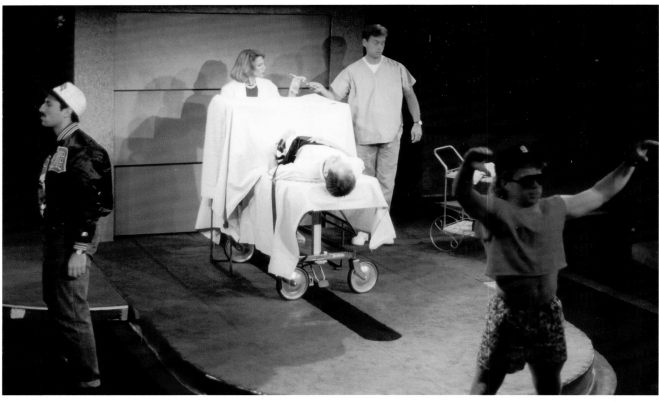

The Vast Difference (1994).

classic dramas over comedies: William Inge's *Bus Stop* (1994), *The Glass Menagerie* (2005), *A Streetcar Named Desire* (2009); Thornton Wilder's *Our Town* (2010); Ernest Thompson's *On Golden Pond* (2012); and Robert Harling's *Steel Magnolias* (2015). Noel Coward's *Blithe Spirit* (2003), and Neil Simon's *The Odd Couple* (2016) are the two classic comedies performed at the Purple Rose.

With mounting theater costs and an increasing number of entertainment options available on television screens, few theaters choose to gamble on new plays. The Purple Rose is an exception. "We pride ourselves on the number of world premieres we produce," the director says. "New plays are the riskiest thing we can undertake. We have to establish a new brand every time, and there's nothing riskier than that. Dramas add another dimension to the decision. We know that comedy sells more quickly, and we love comedy, but only when we can present it as a mirror into the human heart. I'm not the first to say, 'Dying's easy, comedy's hard.' Comedy is certainly not easier to direct than drama. Whatever play we choose, we're here to mess with the way people think and breathe."

Daniels' sixteen (to date) plays and Lanford Wilson's five plays number among Sanville's career milestones as a director, but he is especially proud of *Escanaba in da Moonlight* (1995, 1997, 2011), *Book of Days* (1998), *Rain Dance*, (2001), and *The Vast Difference* (2013), for which he also understudied for the role of the father. He cites his performance in William Mastrosimone's *A Stone Carver* (2012) as his finest work as an actor.

"*Escanaba in da Moonlight* was the first play I directed as A.D.," he explains. "I'm a Yooper from Escanaba, so directing a play about the kind of people I know was a thrill. Many of my family members and friends came down to see it—and for some, that was the first time they had ever been in a professional theater." The play had legs; it was performed in Detroit to sold-out audiences and became a movie starring Jeff Daniels in 2001.

Sanville became the first director in thirty years, with the exception of Marshall Mason, to direct a world premiere professional production of a full-length play written by Lanford Wilson (*Book of Days*, 1998). In 2003, he took the Purple Rose cast that had performed Wilson's *Rain Dance* to New York for an Off-Broadway production Sanville directed. The timing was difficult for the Sanville family because Guy's father was dying, but his family convinced him that his father would have wanted him to take the opportunity.

Guy Sanville often uses the phrase "Bleeding Purple" to describe the passion shared by everyone associated with the Purple Rose.

Guy Sanville plays an aging Italian widower in A Stone Carver *(2012), a role he believes was his finest. "I love playing fathers," he says. He won a Wilde Award for Best Actor.*

Actor/Director Lab 2005

"THE PURPLE ROSE IS A FAMILY...
THE THEATER IS A CALLING FOR US
ALL, A VERY SPECIAL PLACE."

Set in a cantina outside Los Alamos, New Mexico in 1945, immediately following the atomic bomb test, *Rain Dance* explores the psyche of a refugee from Hitler's Germany and three others who have serious concerns about what the Manhattan Project means to the future. *Book of Days* alternates between comedy and tragedy as it unravels a poignant murder mystery that reveals the characters who populate the fictional town of Dublin, Missouri.

Jeff Daniels' *The Vast Difference* is both a comedy and social commentary about a man's mid-life crisis and America's changing views about masculinity. In 1993, Sanville played the ghost of a father. "I love playing fathers," he says. "Many people came up to me afterwards to talk about their husbands and fathers, and I realized I could change people's lives if I did my job well." When the Purple Rose offered the same play twenty years later, Sanville directed and reviewers focused on his successful handling of the material: "Guy Sanville…can move people around a stage in a tango-like dance," wrote Tom Helma in the *Lansing City Pulse*. "The evening unfolds as a sheer delight."

In *A Stone Carver*, Sanville took the part of an ornery Italian father who refuses to be evicted from his home after his wife dies. Helma pointed out, "It takes an actor with great range to project the nuances of a well-written script. Behold the pairing in *A Stone Carver*, by epic-writer William Mastrosimone, which demonstrates the talents of Purple Rose Theater's (sic) artistic director Guy Sanville. It's a marriage of mind and heart made in, if not heaven, at least…Sicily." He continued, "Sanville brings a native intensity to his role….He convincingly portrays an increasingly drunk, paranoid Sicilian…His lines are infused with passion." Sean Dalton, in a review for Heritage.com, wrote, "Guy Sanville breathes life into the character Agostino—or perhaps the more apropos term would be 'new life'…All three members of this very tight cast give the very best performances I've seen." Guy Sanville won a Wilde Award for Best Actor for the role.

A member of the Actors' Equity Association, Screen Actors Guild, and Stage Directors and Choreographers Society, he continues to act once or twice every five years—"I don't really miss acting," he says, "I'm a director by trade. If I act here, we have to agree that I'm the best actor for the part. I know that acting does makes me a better director."

When Sanville plays the role of Oscar in *The Odd Couple* during the winter of 2016, he will turn the role of director over to Resident Artist and former apprentice Lauren Knox. Later in the 25th season, Resident Artist and Literary Manager Michelle Mountain will direct *Morning's At Seven*. "I get résumés from directors all the time, but very few of them have any idea how to make a Purple Rose show." Sanville says. "Guest directors have to do everything I tell them. When I started here, Jeff Daniels was that guy. When he got comfortable with me—around 1998, 1999—he turned the role over to me. We're all still learning."

Since 1998, seven Purple Rose productions of new American plays have been nominated for the George and Mimi Steinberg Award for the Best New Play Produced Outside New York City. In 1998, the PRTC production of *Book of Days* won that award. Jeff Daniels came in second, behind legendary playwright Arthur Miller, for his play *Across the Way* (2002). No other American theater can make that claim over the same period.

In May 2015, the theater filled with friends and family members to commemorate Guy Sanville's twentieth anniversary as Artistic Director. He often uses the phrase "Bleeding Purple" to describe the passion shared by everyone associated with the Purple Rose, and he discussed its meaning that night. "All of us are here in the service of Jeff's vision," he told the audience. "He has always been very clear about his goals: to perform new plays or offer very new approaches to excellent plays, and to develop, nurture, and promote local talent. The

"I have a rich and full fantasy life, and I use it to fuel my fire. I also have a muse, who will always tell me the truth. There is only one person I'm trying to impress. Somewhere along in life, you find that person."

Thy Kingdom's Coming (1994).

"WHATEVER PLAY WE CHOOSE,

WE'RE HERE TO MESS WITH THE WAY

PEOPLE THINK AND BREATHE."

Purple Rose is a family. I have met some of the most decent people I've ever known here. The theater is a calling for us, a very special place. We work very hard every day to give people the opportunity to do their best work. We want to spoil people, so they feel they've had one of the best work experiences of their lives."

"There are six things that actors want from a director: Strong, positive leadership. Organization. Praise. Teaching. Discipline. Kindness."

Director Guy Sanville and Resident Artist Michelle Mountain prepare for the production of Gravity *(2010).*

As the lunch break ends and the Directors' Workshop resumes, Sanville says, "I'm sixty-one and I've been in show business a long, long time. Whenever I meet a playwright—and I've met plenty—I ask what they look for in a director. Everyone says the same thing: 'Someone who's good with actors.'"

After fielding questions from a cluster of apprentices, he rises from his chair with some last-minute thoughts. "There are six things that actors want from a director: Strong, positive leadership. Organization. Praise—the more you give, the more effort they will give you. Teaching. Discipline. Kindness. The best directors help everybody. Trying to teach someone to direct is very, very difficult. A director must have the eye of a painter, a muse, a vivid imagination, and a deep understanding of the way stories work and the dramatic structure of great plays."

Only four hundred men and women in America have a job like his, he adds. "It's a lonely job. A director has to make decisions that might stand in the way of friendships, but you make those decisions for the good of the theater and the actors. The more successful someone is in this business, the lonelier he is. At the end of every day I ask myself: Did I do right by my family? Did I do right by the theater? Did I do right by the people who work with me? If I can answer yes to those questions, it's a great day." ■

The Director

A director must have the eye of a painter, a muse, a vivid imagination, and a deep understanding of the way stories work and the dramatic structure of great plays."

Across the Way 2002

Apartment 3A 1996

33 Variations 2013

The Meaning of Almost Everything 2013

Hope For Corky 2003

"I'm not the first to say that the play's The Thing. And the theater needs talented playwrights to do The Thing justice. It took us ten years to gather a stable of gifted local playwrights. Meanwhile, I jumped in to help fill the gap." —JEFF DANIELS

CHAPTER 3

THE PLAY

Alex Leydenfrost starred in David MacGregor's play Gravity *(2010).*

Opposite page: Scene from Guest Artist *(2006).*

Love. Loss. Friendship. Family. Marriage. Trust. Materialism. Ruptures. Reunions. Hope. Joy. Kindness. Goodness. Evil. Sacrifice. Sacrilege. Secrets.

These are just a handful of the Truths of the human condition that have twirled, tiptoed, and tramped, slithered, schemed, careened, and screeched, whispered, whined, marched, and scuffled across the Purple Rose stage in the forms of comedy, drama, and dramedy.

"Our professional aim is to bring world premieres of outstanding new American plays to the Great Lakes Region," Guy Sanville says. "From the start, Jeff clearly outlined his goals: to provide opportunities for local talent to entertain the wide collective of people who call the Midwest—not New York or LA—home. We also produce classic American plays by seasoned masters—but only if we can do that in fresh and original ways."

The Purple Rose has staged sixty world premieres, nineteen Michigan or Midwest premieres, and sixteen plays by Jeff Daniels. Repeat playwrights include David MacGregor, with four plays performed in Chelsea; Carey Crim, Joan Ackermann, and Kim Carney, who each wrote three scripts for the Purple Rose; and Dennis North, Don Zolidis, Mitch Albom, and Matt Letscher, who wrote two Purple Rose works.

"New plays are the riskiest thing we can do, which is why precious few theaters undertake them," Sanville says. "We establish a new brand every time we do a world premiere. We love comedy, but we don't do comedies exclusively—Gregory Peck and Jack Lemmon were both quoted saying, 'Dying's easy. Comedy's hard.' Whatever play we choose, our goal is to mess with the way people breathe, to entice/urge/encourage them to think different thoughts."

"We work hard to balance comedy and drama, world premieres and classics."

—GUY SANVILLE

Guy Sanville, Lanford Wilson, and Jeff Daniels collaborated on the world premiere professional production of Wilson's play Book of Days *(1998).*

The Purple Rose has also staged classic favorites: Noel Coward's *Blithe Spirit*, Neil Simon's *The Good Doctor*, Steve Martin's adaptation of Carl Sternheim's *The Underpants*, Tennessee Williams' *Glass Menagerie* and *A Streetcar Named Desire*, William Inge's *Bus Stop*, Thornton Wilder's *Our Town*, Ernest Thompson's *On Golden Pond*, and Robert Harling's *Steel Magnolias*. Neil Simon's *The Odd Couple* was scheduled for the 25th season, with Guy Sanville playing Oscar.

"We have stacks and stacks of play submissions every year, but we only produce four plays per season," Sanville says. "Michelle Mountain has become our literary manager. She reads every play that's submitted and passes the possibilities on to me. I always have six new plays in various stages of development and several more in my back pocket. We work hard to balance comedy and drama, world premieres and classics."

The art of playwriting is unique to every writer. After the production of Jeff Daniels' wildly successful play *Panhandle Slim and The Oklahoma Kid* in 2008, the playwright and his director discussed their joint creative process. Ben Daniels taped the conversation.

GUY SANVILLE: *Where did the idea for **Panhandle Slim** come from?*

JEFF DANIELS: I always wanted to write a play for two actors, ever since I saw *Stones In His Pockets*, which is a wonderful Irish play. I saw it on Broadway with two actors playing twenty-five roles, and I said, "Why didn't I write that?" So I decided to write my version….In fact, I wrote about six versions, a complete plagiarism, a complete steal. None of them worked. That was in the spring of 2006…

I had been doing a play in New York called *Blackbird*. There were two characters in that play, and I thought to myself, "What if the actors just stopped doing the play—which is completely unprofessional—and instead they did their own versions without a script? What if that became the play?" I wrote it. It read like a ninety-minute *Saturday Night Live* sketch—and there's a reason why those things are only five to seven minutes long! But you were very kind, Guy. You said, "It needs a lot of work." That's the signal that what you're really saying is, "This isn't going to be good enough."

So I went away for a couple of months and did a movie and went on a band tour with my son Ben….I was driving through Norman, Oklahoma, looking out the window at the prairie, and I returned to the idea of a two-character play. I said, "This is where those two guys are. One's an outlaw. What if I put some music in it? How could I possibly do that if I was going to put it in, say, the 1890s, and make a Western?"

I returned home with notes on February first. You had told me you needed something by February 25.

GS: *I immediately put on the CD of the demo you'd done….I read it and played the songs, then read it again and played the songs. I was absolutely blown away and terrified at the same time. I'd been asking you for a musical and here it was…The way music is integrated into the piece is amazing. The songs actually move the story forward, revealing something about the play. It was very exciting.*

JD: We had John Seibert, an actor who could play the guitar in a basic way. He worked on the guitar for three months, finger-picking, in preparation for the role.

GS: *You wrote this play with two specific actors in mind.*

JD: Yes, for John Seibert and Tom Whalen, which is a wonderful opportunity for a playwright. This is what the Circle Repertory Theatre did. They looked at their acting company, thought about an idea, let it marinate, and all of a sudden there's this play they've written with a part specifically for you…It's like tailoring a suit: the playwright [considers] the actors' strengths and the things he thinks they can do. Perhaps they haven't done them yet, but the potential is there. Certain playwrights—like Lanford Wilson, who is a mentor of mine—work best that way….

"The Circle Repertory Theatre…looked at their acting company, thought about an idea, let it marinate, and all of a sudden there's this play …with a part specifically for you…It's like tailoring a suit."

—JEFF DANIELS

Jeff Daniels wrote Panhandle Slim and the Oklahoma Kid (2008) *specifically for actors Tom Whalen and John Seibert, pictured here with actress Jessica Garrett.*

"To use humor as a window into the human heart is very difficult and takes a lot of courage." —GUY SANVILLE

So, I brought the play in, you read it, and thankfully it was deemed worthy. But you had a suggestion: "Let's blow it up a little bit, let's expand it." I was like, "Oh, God, I was trying to write for two actors and now you're suggesting more." But you were right. There were times the actors were talking, and you said, "Let's not talk about that. Let's show it." So we added another actor in the role of Annabelle…And the changes sent the play over the top. They were great…

I rewrote that play in ten days…and into rehearsal you went.

GS: *The language of the play is…very authentic. Conceptually, that was the way we wanted to approach the piece. The play opens with one guy hogtied and left alone in the desert. We started with this image of blood in the sand. Gradually and powerfully, the motivations and objectives of these characters become so clear and complex….You find yourself wondering—I know I did the first time I read it—"What the hell's going on?" Slowly, life is oozing out of him as the play explores the idea that there is goodness in the worst of us.*

JD: It was the central question for me, the thing that kept me writing, the thing a playwright tries to explore from both sides: Is there goodness in the worst of us? Is there evil even in the good among us? It was fun to explore those questions and come to some kind of spiritual ending.

GS: *I think some of your best work is all about that exploration of good and evil.*

Another playwright was blown away when she saw the play. She said, "It takes so much courage to write from the heart. It takes so much courage to write about things that make people feel something." And that's really true.

It's not hard, I think, to shake someone up about some controversial issue and bombast—or bombard—them with some bold idea or issue, but to shake someone to the core through their heart, to use humor as a window into the human heart, is very difficult and takes a lot of courage.

That comes through with spades in this play—and in all your best work. Right now people are hungry for that.

JD: When you directed this thing, did you do anything different?

GS: *No, we stick to our principles in terms of how we make a play work.*

JD: One of the first and best things you told me, as a director to a playwright, is, "I don't even read the stage directions." Now, that annoyed me because those [outline] how I want you to direct the play. Then I told myself, "Wait a minute." I could see that whatever you guys were doing—and it was something completely different from what I intended—was better. So, I cut 'em all out. There are no parentheticals—"He said incredulously" or "He said laughing" or "Still angry." Now the most I'll put in is, "Enters" or "Goes off." That's it.

Arthur Miller said, "I look forward to seeing what my work inspires in others," and I understand that. It's hard to get to that place, but it's the place all really good playwrights hope to achieve. They want to work with somebody who knows how to lift their work to a higher level. Playwrights give directors the blueprint, and if they give them a good blueprint, directors will probably build something pretty close to what the playwrights intended—but better.

That's where having good people around you is critically important. It's death for a playwright if he or she dictates what actors and directors should do. And that's not how we do things here at the Purple Rose.

GS: *A good example is a key moment in this play, when Panhandle Slim commits a murder. In the script, you say he shoots the man five times. That, to me, when I read the play, was the reason I said, "We should show this." He speaks very eloquently about how awful this guy is, but this scene could offer our one chance to show just how horrible he was.*

JD: Which is a wonderful contrast, because up until then, he was the singing cowboy.

GS: *That was an opportunity to really grab people. It's a beautiful setup for what comes after that….It really earns the ending, which is one of the most beautiful things I've ever seen on stage.*

JD (laughing): There aren't a lot of plays where two actors "climb" onto a horse and ride off into the sunset. I knew I had an ending, I just had to write towards that.

GS: *It's pretty great to see. The audience just delights in that. Seeing adults pretend that way is our idea of a Purple Rose special effect, isn't it?*

JD: (Laughs) Yeah, it is. It's quite elaborate for us.

LANFORD WILSON

"The name Lanford Wilson has special meaning to the Purple Rose Theatre," Guy Sanville says, brandishing a dog-eared, highlighted, and underlined copy of Phillip Middleton Williams' book *A Comfortable House: Lanford Wilson, Marshall W. Mason, and the Circle Repertory Theatre.* "We've performed five of his plays here—two of them world premieres—and we've followed the maxims he helped establish at the Circle Rep."

Wilson was one of the founders of the Off-Off-Broadway theater movement in New York during the mid-1960s. His earliest plays, written in a one-act form, were first produced at the renowned Caffe Cino, beginning in 1964. The following year he teamed with director Marshall Mason, who became his long-time collaborator, to produce *Balm in Gilead.*

Wilson won the Pulitzer Prize for Drama in 1980 for his play *Talley's Folly,* which was performed at the Purple Rose in the spring of 2015. In 2001, he was elected to the Theater Hall of Fame, and in 2004 to the American Academy of Arts and Letters, the same year he received the PEN/Laura Pels International Foundation for Theater Award as a Master American Dramatist. He won five Obie Awards, a Drama Desk Award, and was nominated for three Tony Awards.

"Stylistically," the *New York Times* wrote, "the distinguishing hallmark of Mr. Wilson's work was his dialogue—authentic, gritty, often overlapping….To audiences, his approach gave the experience of eavesdropping on real, bustling people in real, bustling time….Thematically, his work concerned dissolutions large and small: the rupture of societies, families, and individual marriages; the loss of life, love, companionship, and sanity."

"It's death for a playwright if he or she dictates what actors and directors should do. And that's not how we do things here at the Purple Rose."

—JEFF DANIELS

Lanford Wilson's Hot L Baltimore *was produced in 1997.*

By the time Jeff Daniels opened the doors to the Purple Rose, Playwright Lanford Wilson had become the theater's godfather.

Before Jeff Daniels moved to New York at the age of twenty-one, he had performed in Wilson's *Hot L Baltimore* under Marshall Mason's direction. Mason told the young actor that Wilson's approach to his craft was considered "lyric realism." Wilson himself explained, "I wanted to examine real time and real life and see if I could carry and sustain…that specific challenge."

By the time Daniels opened the doors to the Purple Rose, Wilson had become the theater's godfather. His Circle Repertory Theatre had provided a role model for developing talent and producing plays; he himself provided guidance, direction, and encouragement to the fledgling theater. To date, the Purple Rose has presented five of his works: *Hot L Baltimore* (1997), the world premiere of his *Book of Days* (1997), the world premiere of *Rain Dance* (2001), *Redwood Curtain* (2014), and *Talley's Folly* (2015). Upon his death in 2011, Wilson left the PRTC a bequest of $300,000.

"I can't begin to describe the impact Lanford has had on my career and the Purple Rose process," Jeff Daniels says.

A large ensemble performed in Lanford Wilson's Book of Days *1998.*

2AZ (2015) showcased the talents of (l-r) Playwright Michael Brian Ogden, Tom Whalen, David Bendena, Nina White, Drew Parker, and Lauren Knox.

MICHAEL BRIAN OGDEN

Like Jeff Daniels, Michael Brian Ogden pinpoints sixth grade as the time when he realized his future calling. The Resident Artist and author of three plays whose world premieres were staged at the Purple Rose, Ogden says he grew up "pretty nerdy, a kid who loved playing pretend, having adventures as G.I. Joe or Indiana Jones, and turning the school playground into a battlefield where my buddies and I fought Nazis." In sixth grade, he and a friend launched writing/art careers when they convinced their English teacher to give them extra credit for working on comic books—"shameless rip-offs," he says with a grin.

"I GREW UP PRETTY NERDY, A KID WHO LOVED PLAYING PRETEND, HAVING ADVENTURES AS G.I. JOE."

—Michael Brian Ogden

"When I sit down to write, I ask myself what kind of a play I'd like to go see, what someone who is not a regular theatergoer might have an interest in watching."

—MICHAEL BRIAN OGDEN

During his sophomore year in Berkley (MI) High School, he tried out for *The Late Great Me*, and was shocked to learn that he had landed the lead role. He knew at once that he had found his calling. He graduated from Western Michigan University in 2004 with a degree in theater and the drafts of two plays that would eventually appear in revised forms on the Purple Rose stage. He earned certification in stage fighting at the University of Nevada/Las Vegas, and studied theater on the graduate level at Wayne State University, winning a playwriting contest for *Bleeding Red*, which was showcased in Detroit in 2007.

"In a stunning turn of events, Guy Sanville and Michelle Mountain decided to come see what new playwrights were doing that night," Ogden says with a grin. "Guy came up to me and said he'd like me to audition at the Purple Rose." Several years later, Sanville called and asked how many characters *Bleeding Red* features.

"Four and a voice on an answering machine," Ogden told him.

"Okay, we'll take it—if we can have the world premiere here," Sanville told him.

The story of an avid Liverpool soccer fan premiered in 2009, followed by the tale of a Boston hitman in *Corktown*, in 2011, and the dystopian zombie thriller *2AZ* in 2015.

"When I sit down to write, I ask myself what kind of a play I'd like to go see, what someone who is not a regular theater-goer might have an interest in watching," Ogden says. "I've got to see the story in my head before I begin. Some writers like to have their endings first. For me, writing is easiest when I can find an opening moment that has natural momentum. Then I build in complications. I write with two percent instinct and ninety-eight percent luck," he admits. "I'm an actor first and a writer second. I grope for scenes and dialogue that feel right. Acting is much more instinctual for me."

At the close of 2AZ in the summer of 2015, Ogden and his wife Stephanie Buck left Michigan for New York City "with a lot of hope and a few connections." But he intends to maintain his status as Resident Artist.

"Passionate. Dedicated. Generous. Those are the words that come to mind when I think of the Purple Rose," he says. "It taught me to believe in myself. The Purple Rose has a system, and it works. What they do, they do very well."

DAVID MACGREGOR

A Detroit native and Michigan State University graduate, David MacGregor has written plays that have been performed in theaters from California to London. The Purple Rose has featured four of his works: *The Late Great Henry Boyle* (2006), *Vino Veritas* (2008), *Gravity* (2010), and *Consider the Oyster* (2011).

In a glowing review, the *Detroit Free Press* wrote, "The cleverly executed 'Vino Veritas,' about two middle-age couples and an honesty-inducing bottle of wine, speaks directly and profoundly about marriage, child-rearing, career choices, even the existence of God. It also made me laugh—hard." *The Ann Arbor News* added, "The final scene in particular feels like a rare, perfect gem of a moment."

After its premiere at the PRTC, *Vino Veritas* enjoyed a sold-out run during the Nebraska Repertory Theatre's 2009 season. Four years later, an independent film based on *Vino Veritas* was released, starring Carrie Preston and Bernard White.

"I write in my basement—it's just me and my laptop in a totally insulated and isolated environment," MacGregor says. "When I hand my work over to Guy, it's a blueprint of a play. It's the first step. To see what others bring to the play is a fascinating process. It's really, really gratifying to be a part of that."

One of his greatest moments as a playwright happened when he was listening to a soliloquy from *Consider the Oyster,* he says. "The actor nailed it—and I cried at the poignancy of what he was saying. Then I looked two rows back and saw Guy Sanville crying. Life as a playwright doesn't get much better than that."

MacGregor has also sold or optioned screenplays and won screenwriting awards from the American Cinema Foundation and *Fade In* Magazine. He was chosen as one of ten finalists in the 2001 Motion Picture Academy's Nicholl Fellowship Competition, and his screenplay *Shadowplayers* was optioned by Fishbowl Films.

THE PLAY

Opposite page:
M. Brian Ogden has played many roles,
from disillusioned teen (Bleeding Red 2009)
to a hitman,(Corktown 2011) on the
PRTC stage.

Playwright David MacGregor

"When I hand my work over to Guy, it's a blueprint of a play. It's the first step."

—DAVID MACGREGOR

Vino Veritas (2008) starred Quetta Carpenter, Phil Powers, Suzi Regan, and Tommy A. Gomez.

Playwright/Actor Carey Crim auditioned at the PRTC with monologues she wrote.

In addition to writing, MacGregor teaches writing and film classes at Wayne State University. He has been a respondent for the American College Theatre Festival, sponsored by the Kennedy Center.

CAREY CRIM

Originally an actor, Carey Crim found her calling as a playwright by accident—thanks to the Purple Rose Theatre. "I was in Los Angeles for a while," she says, "I did the rounds on a couple of television projects, then spent time in London at the Royal Court Theatre. I came back home to Michigan on what was supposed to be a pit stop at the Purple Rose Theatre Company. When I went to the audition, I had written my own monologues—even though you're not supposed to do that."

She made up the names of the plays and the writers, she said, "and I ended up getting better feedback on the monologues than the actual performances….I came clean and confessed that I had created them. The director asked me if I'd ever write an entire play because he'd like to read it." She sent it to the Purple Rose Theatre for feedback, and Guy Sanville ended up producing *Growing Pretty*.

The Purple Rose also introduced Crim to the works of Lanford Wilson, and she credits Wilson as being one of her professional role models. "Lanford Wilson—probably unknowingly—became a mentor of mine by just letting me watch him work," she says. "He would work right up until his plays premiered. And if he could be that way with his work, I told myself, who am I not to look at my plays from every angle?"

A graduate of Northwestern University, Carey Crim studied at the Royal Court Theatre in London before making her Purple Rose acting debut in 1998. Ten years later, her first play, *Growing Pretty*, held its world premiere at the Purple Rose, followed shortly afterwards by two more world premieres: *Wake* (2009) and *Some Couples May...*(2011).

Wake was optioned for a film, which began shooting in the fall of 2014. Her screenplay *Green Dot Day* was named as a finalist for the 2011 Heideman Award and won the Miami City Theatre's inaugural national short play competition. *Glamping* was a finalist for the same award. Her play *Conviction* premiered at Bay Street Theater and the Rubicon Theater, starring Sarah Paulson and Elizabeth Reaser.

MATTHEW LETSCHER

Like Guy Sanville, Grosse Pointe native and University of Michigan alumnus Matt Letscher appeared in Jeff Daniels' *The Tropical Pickle*. For Letscher, however, it was his first acting role. "Matt impressed me so much that I encouraged him to move to L.A., and while he was out there, I arranged a meeting with Ron Maxwell, director of *Gettysburg*. Matt got a small role in the movie," Daniels says.

Letscher again shared the screen with Daniels in the *Gettysburg* prequel *Gods and Generals*. He has also appeared in *The Mask of Zorro*; *The Beach Boys: An American Family*; *Good Morning, Miami*; *Joey*; *The New Adventures of Old Christine*; *The West Wing*; *CSI Miami*; *Eli Stone*; *Entourage*; *The Carrie Diaries*; *Boardwalk Empire*; *CSI:* and *The Flash*. Along the way, he followed Jeff Daniels' lead and established a second career, as a playwright.

In 2007, the Purple Rose staged the world premiere of Letscher's first script, *Sea of Fools*, a farce set in Hollywood during the Joseph McCarthy era. Daniels originally planned to direct the play, but his schedule forced him to pull out, and Letscher replaced him as director. In 2010, Letscher co-wrote (with Nipper Knapp and Andrew Newberg) the pilot *Gentrification*, which won best writing at the Comedy Central New York Television Festival. A thoughtful exploration of what characteristics and habits humans pass down through the generations, his play *Gaps in the Fossil Record* is one of four plays celebrating the Purple Rose's 25th anniversary season; it won the 2015 Edgerton Foundation New American Play Award soon after the season was announced.

In 2007, the Purple Rose staged the world premiere of (Matthew) Letscher's first script, *Sea of Fools*, a farce set in Hollywood.

Matt Letscher got his first acting role in The Tropical Pickle *and his first film role in* Gettysburg. *Here he directs* Sea of Fools, *the play he wrote.*

"Be you designer, director, performer, or apprentice, your job is to make the play better." —MATT LETSCHER

Matt Letscher, Lanford Wilson, Jeff Daniels, and Guy Sanville work together on the script for Rain Dance (2001).

"No place in my experience offers quite what the Purple Rose does," Letscher says. "The playwright is king/queen at the Purple Rose—not that I wasn't treated beautifully as an actor. You're made to understand that all you do should be in service of the play. And this ethos goes beyond simple platitude, to vigorous, daily practice. Be you designer, director, performer, or apprentice, your job is to make the play better."

The Purple Rose clearly understands that new work is the lifeblood of the American theater, he points out. "They view that as a responsibility as much as a business practicality. In organizations that take this less seriously, a lax attitude sets in that can manifest in statements from actors along the lines of, " I don't understand this/can't make this work, so come up with something better, playwright." When working at "The Rose" as an actor, the mindset soon becomes "How can I make this work, your highness?

"Clearly, I'm overstating," he says, "but I can say that my experience as a playwright at the Purple Rose did make me feel like royalty. To begin with, the time spent in developing the script before any commitment to produce it was invaluable. Two separate workshops prior to our first day of rehearsal forwarded the play to a point where we knew we had something going in, a major confidence-booster. Then, once in rehearsal, every question was posed, every decision was made under the umbrella of Make The Play Better. This translates to Make The Theatre Better. That kind of diligence is rare in our theatrical landscape, in our country, in this time. It must be fostered. Without creative havens like the Purple Rose, it will not." ■

Marcus Is Walking 1998

The Vast Difference 2013

The Last Romance 2014

PRTC
PRODUCTIONS

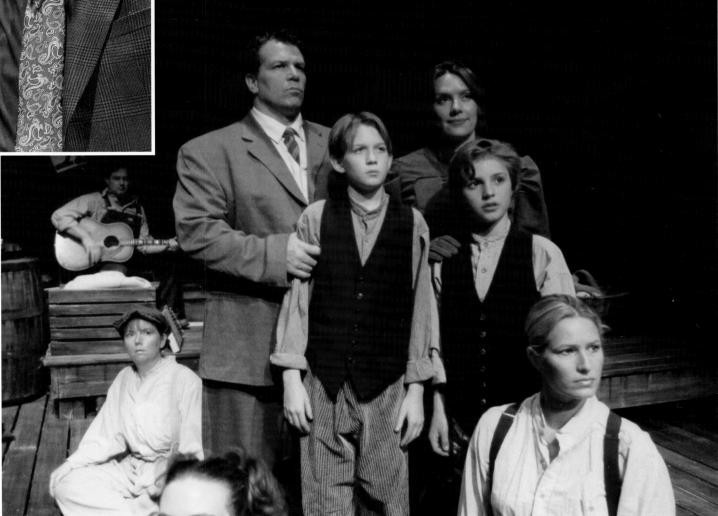

Orphan Train:
An American Melodrama
2001

If you prick us, do we not bleed? if you tickle us, do we not laugh? if you poison us, do we not die? And if you wrong us, shall we not revenge?

—WILLIAM SHAKESPEARE, *MERCHANT OF VENICE*

CHAPTER 4

THE ACTORS

One by one they come. From Chicago, Flint, Detroit, Saginaw, Toledo, Paw Paw, Lansing, Flushing, Pittsburgh, Traverse City, Perryville, South Bend, and Los Angeles. Some rap politely on the door. Others tap timidly or bang defiantly. When they hear Guy Sanville's voice call, "Come in," some saunter, some stride purposefully, some march, tiptoe, or glide. But all are here for the same reason.

The Audition.

Over the course of two very long days and nights, Guy Sanville and Michelle Mountain will listen courteously to nearly 180 actors—some aspiring, some professional—as they perform. Yet the Purple Rose has only two unclaimed roles for the upcoming season, with several understudy parts still available.

Sanville rises, smiles, shakes each actor's hand, introduces Michelle Mountain, then invites, "Sit and tell us something about yourself."

Perched on the edge of the plastic seat, dozens of trained professionals talk about their career highlights; college students discuss their classes; several current apprentices chit-chat about theater business; an elegantly dressed middle-aged woman laments her broken marriage; a soldier describes his deployment in Afghanistan; a high school senior looks blank and admits, "I don't have anything to say. My life hasn't begun yet."

First to appear: Maurice, a Wayne State graduate with a degree in broadcast journalism. "Journalism is another way to exercise my creativity, although performance is my first passion," he says. At Sanville's invitation, he offers a comic monologue about a man trying to decide whether to save his girlfriend or mother as their ship goes down.

"Nice work," Sanville says. "You have enormous potential. Keep at it."

As Maurice leaves the room, Sanville jots an "8" on the actor's profile. His rankings run from one to ten.

Above: Guy Sanville directing.

Opposite page: Lisa Klein auditions for Guy Sanville.

Call-backs give new actors a chance to showcase their talents.

"Directors must find out what actors—and their audience members—know, and then lead them to learn more."

—GUY SANVILLE

Nicole has acted in Chicago. After her comic monologue, Sanville asks for another, "This one serious." He writes an "8" on her résumé.

David has toured with the Michigan Shakespeare Company. In deep and ringing tones, he starts a monologue about a man who has lost his penis. Sanville stops him midway. "Just look at Michelle and tell her a story. Tell her about the best day of your life." David follows the directions, then Sanville says, "Now, do your monologue just like that." After David performs again and exits, the director explains, "Trying to be funny is death. That's why I ask for serious. What we do here is really hard, sophisticated, big-city stuff. If they don't offer that immediately, I have to be confident that I can get them there in two weeks. Otherwise, I can't consider them."

Sometime mid-morning, he asks Emily, a young mother, if she can speak in an upper-class English accent, then a Cockney accent. "I can fix her," the director tells Mountain as the door closes behind Emily. "We can consider her for the understudy role."

A pompous senior from Michigan State comes and goes within four minutes. "There are some people who walk into a room and expand the air, and there are others who suck the air out of it," Sanville says, pulling off his baseball cap and mopping his forehead as day turns into night.

A handsome thirty-something soldier, clean-cut and respectful, says that he has just returned from a deployment. "I've never acted in my life, but it's something I've always wanted to do." When he finishes his monologue, Sanville tells him he's talented. "We've got an acting class that could get you where you want to go," he says. When the captain shows interest, the director suggests, "We'll give you our military discount—and we'll look forward to working with you."

"I didn't know we gave a military discount," Michelle Mountain says after the soldier leaves.

"We do now," Sanville tells her. "He's never had any training, yet he prepared well and knew to look us in the eyes. With a little help, he could go somewhere."

(Within weeks, the soldier was cast as an understudy for the two soldiers in 2AZ.)

Both Sanville and Mountain recognize Ashley, who has auditioned several times. She tells them she's taking voice lessons "because I'm afraid of my own voice." Her monologue is delivered in a pseudo-Southern accent. Sanville suggests a redo. "Talk directly to Michelle," he says. "Lose the accent. The woman I interviewed is so much more interesting than the character she just played. I want to see Ashley tell her story." He nods encouragingly. "You're good! You can do this." She follows the directions and when the audition ends, she leaves with a smile.

Landon, a young James Dean look-alike, auditions with clenched fists and deep, dark tones. When he finishes, Sanville asks, "Do you want to goof around for a minute?"

The young man looks startled. "Okay."

Sanville suggests that Resident Artist Lauren Knox sit at his feet. "Now, use those same words, but just tell Lauren that story," Sanville says. "Hold her hands and don't take your eyes off her when you speak. Don't act. Just tell her the story."

Landon repeats the exercise three times before Sanville tells him, "You've got loads of potential. I'm not trying to sell our fall acting class, but if you're willing, I'll give you one for half-price. You have extraordinary gifts, and we can help you explore them."

When the young man leaves, the director says, "He's the only young, great-looking, charismatic expander male we've had so far. The business eats guys like him alive, but he has a chance for success. I can see him heading off to California and the movie business in a year or two. He has what Hollywood is always looking for."

Sanville believes that between seventy and eighty percent of his job relies on good casting. "We have to have good raw material to work with," he says. "We don't hire assholes, no matter how good they are. We're looking for people with talent who are willing to learn and to work

Michelle Mountain and Alex Leydenfrost perform together in Gravity. *Hundreds of aspiring actors hope to follow in their footsteps.*

Susan Craves began acting in community theater before taking PRTC acting classes. She understudied for several roles before appearing in Steel Magnolias *in 2015.*

hard with us. We take really good care of people here. This theater entertains 40,000 visitors every year. Lots of local businesses depend on us. If I cast someone, I'm betting my mortgage on that person. To maintain the quality of this theater, we need highly skilled and trained professionals."

At the end of the two days, Guy Sanville and Michelle Mountain call back fourteen young women and three men—a record, the director says wearily as he stands, stretches, and gathers his notes. He estimates that 500 actors performed on the Purple Rose stage during its first quarter-century and 2,500 auditioned during that time.

SUSAN CRAVES

A Michelle Mountain look-alike, Susan Craves landed her first Purple Rose role—no surprise—as Mountain's understudy. "Whenever I'm in Chelsea, people will ask, 'Are you—?,'" she says. "Michelle and I have become dear friends." The Purple Rose's newest Resident Artist, Craves earned her equity card in Chelsea serving as Mountain's understudy in *Redwood Curtain*; *The PRTC Spring Comedy Festival: Lovers, Liars, & Lunatics*; and *Annapurna*.

Craves began acting in community theater as a child, but took a long break to fulfill other goals. She was chosen Miss Bay County in 1982, then participated in the 1983 Miss Michigan contest. She earned a degree in fashion merchandising and, later, a teaching certificate. She taught. She became a mother. She worked as a flight attendant. After a while, though, she realized something was missing: "Acting."

She started with community theaters, then moved into roles on professional theater stages. In 2001, she signed up for Guy Sanville's "Acting for the Camera" class at the University of Michigan. She was hooked. She took additional classes and then became an understudy.

"People have asked why I choose to understudy if I can get cast elsewhere," she says. "I tell them that the understudy position at the Purple Rose is more fulfilling. The theater treats understudies so well—we're not thought of as less than lead actors. We know it's an honor. Every time I'm an understudy, I feel as if I'm taking a master's class. I love it."

Purple Rose understudies are required to attend at least fifteen hours of rehearsals and see at least two shows per week. They begin their rehearsals after the show opens. "Before that, we watch closely and take notes," she explains. "In some ways, the understudy's job is harder than preparing for the role as lead actor. I have to follow every nuance Michelle makes. I can't change a thing. I need to make sure that the other actors on stage will be as comfortable with me as they are with her. An understudy can't have an ego." Nor can understudies change their hair color or cut unless they get permission from the stage manager.

Four times Craves filled in for Mountain before her 2015 debut in *Steel Magnolias*, when the fifty-five-year-old happily married woman played a seventy-one-year-old widow. "Obviously, I didn't play myself, but my debut was a dream come true," she says. "I can't even begin to describe what the Purple Rose has done for me and my family. It has been life-changing. It's improved my confidence — if Guy hadn't helped me with that, I never would have auditioned. This theater has introduced me to world-class plays and amazingly talented people. It's given me a career direction I thought I could only dream about."

DAVID DAOUST

Jeff Daniels wrote the comedy *Casting Session* with two PRTC veterans in mind: David Daoust and Tom Whalen. They played middle-aged actors who have been competing for the same roles for thirty years, and they go to unusual lengths to land a juicy part. During the twenty-fifth anniversary season, Daoust was also cast in *Morning's At Seven*, following performances in *White Buffalo*, *Across the Way*, *Born Yesterday*, and *Superior Donuts*, which earned him the Rogue Critic's Best Supporting Actor in a Drama Award.

A Michigan native and Eastern Michigan graduate, he says he stumbled into an acting class taught by the founders of the BoarsHead Theater — "and it changed my life for the better." Daoust jockeyed a job as radio host at WBOC-Radio and TV Park in Salisbury, Maryland with theater roles, some of them Off- and Off-Off Broadway, and appearances in three films: *To Live and Die in Dixie*, *Vito Power*, and *Highland Park*. He has written two one-man shows for school-age audiences, *Jefferson Lives!* and *Jefferson and the Science of the 18th and 19th Century*. A repeat offender on *Law & Order*, he frequently does voice-overs and book recordings.

David Daoust in The Poetry of Pizza *(2007).*

In 2012, Stacie Hadgikosti Mitchell (l) and Rainbow Dickerson starred in White Buffalo, *a Native American story.*

RAINBOW DICKERSON

The daughter of a Thai mother and Native American father, Rainbow Dickerson trained at the East 15 Acting Conservatory at the University of Essex in London, England, and at the Circle in the Square Theatre School in New York. She first appeared in the Purple Rose world premiere of *White Buffalo*, followed by *Redwood Curtain*.

Her career is remarkably varied. She apprenticed to the Art Director/Chief Scenic Artist of the MET, CBS & ABC TV; served as the co-artistic director of the Velocity Theatre Company in New York; and stage managed the Washington (D.C.) Opera Company. She has worked on Broadway (*August: Osage County*), Off-Off Broadway, in regional theaters across the country, and in three films: *Tremendous, Horizon,* and *The World at Night.* Besides certification in both the British and American societies of stage combat, she is proficient in archery, horseback riding, and cooking—she took home the Golden Whisk in the "Super Cake Heroes" series on the Food Network.

SARAB KAMOO

"What I love best about the Purple Rose is the way they love their actors," Sarab Kamoo says. "People there do whatever they can to help you tell the story."

Guy Sanville first saw Kamoo when she performed in *9 Points of Desire*, playing nine Iraqi women offering their perspectives on the war. He invited her to take a look at the PRTC, and after participating in several classes, she was cast in *Marcus is Walking, The Underpants, Consider the Oyster,* and *And The Winner Is.* "I owe Guy Sanville so much," she says. "He's been fundamental in teaching me so many things, giving me so many opportunities at such a young age. His classes provided the framework and backbone of what I use today, and I'm so grateful."

Kamoo earned a bachelor's degree in communications and English and a master's degree in social work. She is a school social worker, so she can make herself available for plays, television, film, and voice-over work.

"Performing is part of my makeup. It's who I am," she says.

LAUREN KNOX

"My mother always told me to follow my dreams—that's the best advice someone can give young people," Lauren Knox says. She followed her dream and found herself in the right place at the right time. Several times.

At Oakland University, she studied theater with a former Purple Rose apprentice who taught acting the way he learned it in Chelsea: *Tell the truth. Make it about your partner. Every scene is a love scene.* At his suggestion, Knox drove to Chelsea for a *Bleeding Red* performance in the winter of 2009. When the play ended that night, she promised herself that one day she, too, would have a play performed at the Purple Rose.

She met *Bleeding Red* author Brian Ogden when they acted in Water Works' *Henry V.* At his suggestion, she applied to the Purple Rose apprenticeship program, but she was told she would have to wait a year and then reapply. "I wasn't sure what my next step should be," she says. "I thought of moving to Seattle or New York, but doors opened and doors closed, so I prayed for opportunities." Soon afterwards, Michelle Mountain left a message on Knox's phone, saying someone had dropped out of the apprenticeship program. Could she start in two weeks? Knox still has that message. "It changed my life."

Sarab Kamoo starred in Consider the Oyster, *a play written by David MacGregor in 2011.*

"Performing is part of my makeup. It's who I am."

—SARAB KAMOO

"I don't believe in coincidences. I do believe in miracles—big and little ones—and the Purple Rose has provided me with both."

—LAUREN KNOX

Almost immediately, more doors opened. Guy Sanville told her he had heard from people he trusted that she was a good actor. When a stage manager couldn't read stage directions at a Chelsea District Library reading, Lauren was asked to fill in. She heard Guy Saville laughing at her lines—"That was a highlight," she says. But there was more to come.

When her apprentice rotation landed her in the house manager position ("which involves cleaning the theater and bathrooms before and after performances"), an actor dropped out of 33 *Variations* and her understudy couldn't take her place full-time. Sanville asked Knox to step in. She acted in every performance while fulfilling her apprenticeship duties. Later, she served as understudy for both sisters in *Miles and Ellie*.

When Knox's apprenticeship ended, Sanville offered her a directing apprenticeship for *Annapurna*, warning, "Tell me what you think, not what you think I want to hear." She took his advice. Later that year, she starred in *2AZ*, and was tapped to direct her director in *The Odd Couple* in 2006.

"I truly believe that I wouldn't be where I am today if it hadn't been for prayer and God's hand over my life," she says. "I don't believe in coincidences. I do believe in miracles—big and little ones—and the Purple Rose has provided me with both."

BRIAN LETSCHER

Brian Letscher graduated from the University of Michigan with an economics degree and the thrill of having played football in the Big House. After college, he moved to New York City to pursue acting, starting with training at the Public Theater Shakespeare Lab. He quickly landed roles in movies (*Kate and Leopold, Puccini for Beginners*), television (*Law and Order: CI, SVU*) and theater. He played the lead in the PRTC's *Bus Stop*, which won the *Detroit Free Press* Best Play Award. Following in his brother Matt's shoes, he began playwriting. The Purple Rose produced the world premiere of his first effort, *When the Lights Come On*, which is based on his football career at the University of Michigan.

Opposite page: top
During her apprenticeship, Lauren Knox appeared onstage in 33 Variations (2013).

Opposite page: bottom
Brian Letscher played the lead in Bus Stop (2005).

Left: After appearing in Jeff Daniels' play The Tropical Pickle (2002), *Matt Letscher was cast in* Gettysburg, *thanks to Daniels' introduction.*

Since moving to California, Letscher has guest-starred in more than a dozen prime-time television shows (among them ABC's *Scandal* and NBC's *Crisis*). He performs with the Pacific Residents Theatre Company and continues his playwriting.

MATT LETSCHER

Actor/playwright/University of Michigan alumnus Matt Letscher landed his first professional acting job when Jeff Daniels cast him in *The Tropical Pickle*, along with Guy Sanville. Letscher impressed Daniels enough that he arranged for a meeting with Film Director Ron Maxwell, resulting in a small role in *Gettysburg*. Letscher took his career to Hollywood, but returned to Chelsea to act in the world premiere of Lanford Wilson's play *Rain Dance*.

Redwood Curtain (2014) starred Alex Leydenfrost as a war-scarred veteran, along with Rainbow Dickerson and Michelle Mountain.

The next year, he joined the television comedy *Good Morning, Miami* and performed at the Lincoln Center Theater in *The Rivals*. He was cast in *Joey*, had recurring roles on *The New Adventures of Old Christine* and *The Flash*, and starred in the series *Bent* and *Scandal*. His play *Gaps in the Fossil Record* was the third scheduled for the PRTC twenty-fifth anniversary season.

ALEX LEYDENFROST

Alex Leydenfrost moved to Ann Arbor in 2007, after working in Los Angeles for thirteen years. His first Michigan role, in *Panache* at the Williamston Theatre, won him a 2009 Wilde Award for Best Actor in a Comedy. Purple Rose audiences have enjoyed his performances in

Some Couples May…; *Best of Friends*; *Gravity*; *Wake*; *White Buffalo*; *Superior Donuts*; and *Redwood Curtain*. *Ann Arbor News* reviewer Jenn McKee wrote that Leydenfrost's performance in *Redwood Curtain* "impressively conveyed the pain of an off-the-grid veteran who struggles with basic human interaction."

Previously, Leydenfrost toured Europe with the American Drama Group Europe. As a member of the New Actors Workshop in New York, he studied with Mike Nichols, George Morrison, and Paul Sills. A performing arts teacher in Ann Arbor schools, he has appeared Off-Broadway and in three films: *The Five Spot* (1993), *Have a Little Faith* (2011), and *Pilot Error* (2014).

STACIE HADGIKOSTI MITCHELL

Stacie Hadgikosti Mitchell earned a theater degree from Western Michigan University and a master's degree in acting from Purdue before appearing at the Purple Rose in *Corktown*, *Growing Pretty*, *Boeing-Boeing*, *Our Town*, *Gravity*, *Wake*, *Bleeding Red*, *A Streetcar Named Desire*, and *White Buffalo*. Her film credits include *Mooz-Lum* (2010), *Dogman* (2012), *Dogman 2: The Wrath of the Litter* (2014), and *Opening Night* (2014).

Above: Alex Leydenfrost splits his time between the theater and teaching. Here he stars in Best of Friends *(2010).*

Below left: The story of Isaac Newton's discovery, Gravity *(2010) showcased the talents of an ensemble, including Stacie Hadgikosti Mitchell.*

Over its first twenty-five years, 500 actors have appeared on the Purple Rose stage.

JANET MAYLIE

Janet Maylie's history with the Purple Rose dates back to its earliest days, when she was cast in Jeff Daniels' first play, *Shoe Man* (1991). She acted in six other productions here: *The Vast Difference* (both in Chelsea and at Detroit's Gem Theatre); *The Purple Rose Spring Comedy Festival, Completing Dahlia, Off the Map, Sea of Fools,* and *Blithe Spirit*. Early in her career, she appeared on television in *Hill Street Blues, The Love Boat,* and *As the World Turns,* plus more than ninety commercials, several Off-Broadway productions, and numerous theatrical productions. A faculty member in Michigan's Department of Theatre and Drama, she received four Theatre Excellence Awards from the *Detroit Free Press*.

RUSTY MEWHA'S CAREER ROUTE WAS CIRCUITOUS—IT INVOLVED COLLEGE, DROPPING OUT OF THEATER SCHOOL, QUITTING ACTING, WORKING AS A BLUE-COLLAR TEAMSTER, AND STARTING HIS FAMILY.

RUSTY MEWHA

In junior high school, Rusty Mewha began performing in plays and choirs, inspired by the musical *Les Miserables* and the film *The Dead Poets Society*. "But my career route was circuitous—it involved Wayne State University, dropping out of theater school, quitting acting, working as a blue collar Teamster, and starting my family," he says. It wasn't until the age of twenty-eight that he began taking acting seriously. Since then, he has performed on many professional stages after earning his actor's equity card at the Purple Rose.

On the big screen, Mewha appeared in *Whip It* (2009), *Prayers for Bobby* (2009), *Conviction* (2010), *Red Dawn* (2012), *Highland Park* (2013), and *Liberty's Secret: The 100% All-American Musical* (2016), in which he plays Abraham Lincoln. His PRTC credits include *The PRTC Spring Comedy Festival: Lovers, Liars & Lunatics*; *The Vast Difference*; *Miles & Ellie*; *2AZ*; and *Morning's At Seven*. He understudied for *Honus and Me* and *When the Lights Come On*.

"Jeff Daniels has actually written roles for me! I still get goosebumps thinking about that. I'm very lucky." —MICHELLE MOUNTAIN

MICHELLE MOUNTAIN

"Michelle Mountain is one of the finest actors working today, bar none," Guy Sanville tells actors in his summer Actors' Boot Camp. Her roles reflect his confidence in her: *Best of Friends*; *Boeing-Boeing*; *Our Town*; *Gravity*; *Wake*; *A Streetcar Named Desire*; *The Poetry of Pizza*; *When the Lights Come On*; *The Subject Was Roses*; *The Glass Menagerie*; *Norma & Wanda*; *Blithe Spirit*; *Across the Way*; *Born Yesterday*; *Orphan Train: An American Melodrama*; *The Hole* (for which she won the Detroit Free Press Best Actress Award); *Marcus is Walking*; *33 Variations*; *Book of Days*; *Annapurna*; *Steel Magnolias*; *2AZ*; and *The Odd Couple*. And when she isn't acting, she is teaching, reading scripts, or directing; her PRTC director's credits include *Growing Pretty*, *Hope for Corky*, *On Golden Pond*, *The Last Romance*, and *Morning's At Seven*.

A Wisconsin native, Michelle Mountain knew she wanted to act from a very young age. In kindergarten, she organized the neighborhood kids to perform shows in the family's garage. "I remember coloring my hands and feet blue with food coloring for my appearance as the witch in *Hansel & Gretel*," she says. Years later, her tenth-grade English teacher suggested she try out for the school's production of *Pillow Talk*. Landing the part affirmed her passion for acting.

That led to auditions and three years in Summer Stock, during which she performed in eighteen shows. "I was the youngest and I was terrible, but I got great training," she says. The producer told her he hired her for two reasons: first, she was funny; and, secondly, he said, "She's not the best actress, but she's the easiest to get along with."

Above: Richard McWilliams and Michelle Mountain in Annapurna (2014).

Opposite page: Janet Maylie and Dana Gamarra appeared in Jeff Daniels' first world premiere Shoe Man (1991).

Opposite page: Rust Mewha appears in The Vast Difference (2013).

"That was a lesson I took to heart," Mountain tells acting students. "Being flexible, adaptable, eager to learn, and willing to work hard are all critically important if you want a career in the theater."

She earned her master of fine arts degree in acting at the University of Wisconsin before heading to the University of California at San Diego, where she married her husband (set designer Vince Mountain) and began teaching. The couple moved to Seattle and started their family while Vince pursued a design fellowship and Michelle landed acting and teaching jobs. When Vince was offered the chance to teach at the University of Michigan in 1994, Michelle confesses, "I honestly thought my professional life was over."

But her career actually took off. She found steady work with the Wild Swan Theater and Young People's Theater, then brushed elbows with the Purple Rose for the first time in 1996, when she took Sanville's acting class. He was impressed and offered her an understudy position in *Labor Day*; she appeared onstage when the lead actress became ill. *Book of Days* was the next play on the schedule. When the forty-two-year-old lead actress decided she was too young to play a fifty-two-year-old woman, Guy offered Michelle the role. The thirty-seven-year-old actress jumped at the chance, and the roles kept coming, both at the Purple Rose and in film.

Mountain played Jeff Daniels' wife in the 2002 movie *Super Sucker* and appeared in *Beyond the Pale* (2007), *Frozen Stupid* (2008), and the short *How My Cat Got Murdered* (2015). She serves as the PRTC apprentice chief, literary manager, and director of educational programing; she teaches acting, directing, playwriting, voice, and movement classes.

Reviewers love Mountain's work. Critiquing 33 *Variations* (2013), AnnArbor.com noted, "The show is primarily a showcase for Mountain, who depicts her character's physical deterioration and emotional evolution with skill and care." EncoreMichigan.com reviewed the same show: "Michelle Mountain as Katherine and Richard McWilliams as Beethoven are outstanding…an illustration of the human will's triumph over adversity." Critic Tom Helma wrote, "Actress Michelle Mountain plays the central character…and weaves through the multi-leveled story lines of the play with what looks like an effortless ease combined with a wide range of acting expression. She is loose and spontaneous…[and] does a great job of putting passionate emotion on the stage at all times." The Rogue Critic named her Best Lead Actress in a Drama for that role.

"I've played every role I could imagine, and then some," Mountain says, pinpointing Blanche in *A Streetcar Named Desire* and Billy in *Born Yesterday* as two of many highlights. "I love my job. I love my life," she says. "Jeff Daniels has actually written roles for me! I still get goosebumps thinking about that. I'm very lucky. I work hard. I get better every year and I get to help others learn and grow in their chosen field."

The actor adds, "Jeff Daniels always says, 'You have to be ready because you never know when your two minutes of opportunity might come.' My career is a living example of that. I was ready. I try to teach others to become ready."

Opposite page: The ensemble cast on the set of Born Yesterday (2002) *included Michelle Mountain and Guy Sanville.*

Left: Michael Brian Ogden dreamed of playing G. I. Joe as a young boy. His dream came true in 2AZ (2015), *an apocalyptic play that introduces zombies to the Purple Rose stage.*

Below: Wayne David Parker first appeared on the PRTC stage in The Tropical Pickle (1992), *but his recurring role as da Jimmer in the* Escanaba *series and film made him famous nation-wide.*

MICHAEL BRIAN OGDEN

Michael Brian Ogden is one of the only actors who has appeared on the Purple Rose stage in world premieres of his own plays: *Corktown, Bleeding Red,* and *2AZ.* "Acting is my first love," he says. He has also appeared in twelve other PRTC productions, including *Apartment 3A, Our Town, Escanaba in da Moonlight,* and *Growing Pretty,* as well as two films: *Kill the Irishman* (2011) and *Pilot Error* (2014).

A Western Michigan graduate, he studied acting in the Hilberry Theatre's master of fine arts program at Wayne State University before training with the Moscow Art Theatre and the Society of American Fight Directors. "The Purple Rose means more than I can say. I met my wife [Stephanie Buck] here, they offered me my first professional acting and teaching jobs, gave me my equity card, and taught me my craft."

WAYNE DAVID PARKER

Jeff Daniels' *Escanaba* trilogy became a showcase for Wayne David Parker's talents; he also brought da Jimmer to the movie screen in *Escanaba in da Moonlight* and starred in Daniel's directorial film debut, *Super Sucker,* as well as appearing in a dozen other movies, including *Stone* (2010), where he shares the screen with Robert de Niro, and Mitch Albom's *Have a Little Faith* (2011).

In 2011, Jim Porterfield and Michelle Mountain shared an important milestone: one thousand performances in more than twenty plays at the Purple Rose.

A veteran of countless regional theaters and two dozen Purple Rose productions, he says his favorite plays include *The Underpants*, *Book of Days*, *Thy Kingdom's Coming*, and *Duck Hunter Shoots Angel*, as well as the Escanaba series. His voice can be heard regularly in radio and television commercials. "I treat each voice-over as a thirty-second or sixty-second play," he says. "I'm a character actor. I enjoy the widely different characters I play."

JIM PORTERFIELD

In 2011, Jim Porterfield and Michelle Mountain shared an important milestone: one thousand performances in more than twenty plays at the Purple Rose. "Jim and Michelle are two of the best actors in the country—but they're two of the best actors most people outside Chelsea have never heard of. They're world class," Guy Sanville said at the time.

Escanaba in da Moonlight, *Honus and Me*, *Book of Days*, *Some Couples May...*, *Our Town*, and *Gravity* are among the plays that have showcased Porterfield's talents. A graduate of Michigan State, his movie credits include *Barn Red*, *Frozen Stupid*, *Prayers for Bobby*, and *Kill the Irishman*. He appeared in the TV series *Detroit 1-8-7* and the TV movie *Last Man Standing*. Acting shares time with his other passion: trees. He is the president of Porterfield Tree Service.

Yooper adventures in a hunting cabin showcased the comedic skills of Jim Porterfield (l) and Matthew David (r) in Escanaba in da Moonlight *(2011).*

Rhiannon Ragland played a nurse-turned-vigilante in the dystopian play 2AZ *(2015).*

RHIANNON RAGLAND

Rhiannon Ragland first visited the Purple Rose to see *The Subject Was Roses,* starring Michelle Mountain, Grant Krause, and Patrick Michael Kenney. She remembers a moment between father and son that was "so volatile, so uncomfortable, and so close to home" that she thought she would have to leave the theater. "Those performances were so jarring, so utterly truthful that they physically hurt to watch. They were an awe-inspiring example of great acting," she recalls.

Her mother, a producer and actor who attended PRTC open auditions in 2005, encouraged her daughter to train here. Rhiannon took her advice and took classes for a year and a half before she got her break, when an actress bowed out of Brian Letscher's play *When the Lights Come On.* "I went through three auditions for that role," Ragland says. "Up until that point, acting at the Purple Rose was a pipe dream. I never believed it would actually come true."

She made her professional debut in 2007, as the wife of an up-and-coming coach. Since then, she has been cast in *Growing Pretty; Escanaba in da Moonlight; Consider the Oyster; Some Couples May…; Best of Friends; Boeing-Boeing; Our Town; Gravity; A Streetcar Named Desire; Apartment 3A; The PRTC Spring Comedy Festival: Lovers, Liars, & Lunatics; On Golden Pond; 33 Variations; The Vast Difference; Miles & Ellie; Steel Magnolias; 2AZ; The Odd Couple;* and *Morning's At Seven.*

Ragland has played everything from an 18th-century housemaid to a stewardess, gun-toting nurse, conflicted career woman, and construction worker.

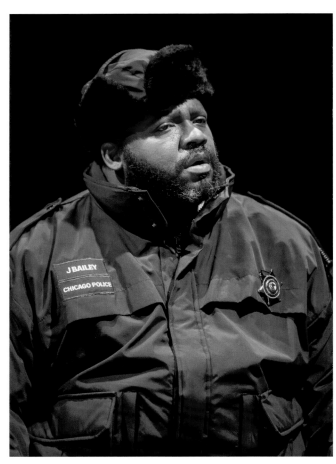

Lynch Travis abandoned a career in managed healthcare in order to devote himself to theater. Here appears in Superior Donuts *(2012).*

Trying to pinpoint a favorite role is like asking a parent which child is the favorite, she says, though she quickly adds that she is especially proud of 2AZ. "Guy Sanville put together the absolute right cast—sixteen of us—at the absolute right time," she says. "From Day One, there was no fooling around. We were all in it together. We saw how hard Guy was working and how much he believed in the play and its message. He was involved in everything from the smallest details of set design to the fight choreography, and that set the bar very high.

"Besides," she adds, laughing, "I don't get many opportunities to kick butt and haul around a shotgun."

Her first lead role came with the 2008 *Apartment* 3A revival. "I knew who had starred in the first production, and I knew the professionalism of the rest of the cast. I was intimidated," she says. "Over and over again, I had to remind myself to 'fire the judge'."

According to Ragland, the pace of the comedy *Boeing-Boeing* posed an unexpected challenge. "We don't often do that kind of comedy at the Rose. It has a musical timing," she explains. "The action is so fast, and yet we're still trying to tell the truth without having it slip away. If anyone took half a breath at the wrong moment, it would throw everyone off. But it was so much fun to perform, and the audience had as much fun with it as we did." She enjoyed her character's idiosyncracies: "I was Italian and sassy and funny."

Her contributions to PRTC productions have gone beyond acting. She directed Guy Sanville in *A Stone Carver*, which won a Wilde Award for Best Drama. She designed the costumes for *Miles & Ellie*. And she worked on the design teams for *White Buffalo* and *The Last Romance*. She also choreographed *The Meaning of Almost Everything*.

When her time isn't consumed by Purple Rose responsibilities, she works in construction, renovating homes. But her heart belongs to the theatre in Chelsea. "Will David Young expressed how I feel about working at the Purple Rose: 'This is the place where you want to work. Everywhere else is where you have to work.' I totally agree," she says. "Here we have the best of the best. Being a Resident Artist here is a gift, and I honor it closely."

LYNCH TRAVIS

"A crazy set of circumstances made me see myself as a professional actor," Lynch Travis says. The economics major participated in theater performances during his college years, but he became an insurance company auditor, abandoning his acting career for fifteen years before auditioning at a community theater in Southfield, Connecticut. After decades in managed healthcare, he decided to take the leap into a full-time acting/directing career. When he relocated to Michigan, he introduced himself to Guy Sanville at the *Detroit Free Press* theater awards in 1999, and Sanville mentioned he had a play that might interest the Detroit actor. That launched a long-standing relationship with the Purple Rose.

His first appearance was in *Orphan Train: An American Melodrama* (2000). "I got a good response, so I decided to hang around," he jokes. He was cast in *Stand*; *Duck Hunter Shoots Angel*; *Escanaba*; and *Superior Donuts*. He also launched a film career, with *Standing in the Shadows of Motown* (2002), *The Butterfly Effect 3: Revelations* (2009), *The Ghost of St. Aubin* (2011), *Dogman* (2012), and *Highland Park* (2013), and he played himself in the television series *Chicago Fire* (2015). Travis teaches and serves as Resident Director for the Blackbird Theatre Company.

TOM WHALEN

Tom Whalen auditioned at the Purple Rose for seven straight years before his first callback, but he quickly became part of the theatrical family. In 2001, he was teaching at Brewster Academy in Wolfborough, New Hampshire, when his friend, playwright Dennis North, told him his play had been optioned by the Purple Rose. Whalen flew to Michigan to audition for *Orphan Train: An American Melodrama*, and Guy Sanville hired him on the spot. That role was quickly followed by *Our Town*; *Escanaba*; *Panhandle Slim and The Oklahoma Kid*; *The Glass Menagerie*; *The Good Doctor*; *Let It Be*; *Guys on Ice*; *The PRTC Spring Comedy Festival: Lovers, Liars, & Lunatics*; *The Vast Difference*; *2AZ*; *Casting Session*; and *The Odd Couple*.

"I've chosen to be closely associated with the Purple Rose because life here is always dynamic, always challenging," he says. Besides acting, he serves as resident sound designer.

Tom Whalen's introduction to a theatrical life started when he was an altar boy in a Catholic church in North Dakota. "I was the kid who always did the gospel readings at church. I'm not sure why," he says. "Maybe I was the only one with chutzpah. But I liked doing it."

In his early twenties, he took a leave of absence from the family business and performed in North Dakota and Minnesota community and regional theaters, as well as on a paddlewheel showboat, where he sang in operettas. He returned to the family business, but in 1983, he decided to pursue acting seriously. He moved to Detroit and enrolled in Wayne State's Hilberry Theatre program. "My intention was to stay in Michigan just until I got my union card. That was thirty years ago," he says.

Since then, he has worked steadily, and when he isn't rehearsing, performing, or designing sound, he drives long-distance rigs. "That job offers a lot of time for rehearsing lines," he says. Long-distance drivers are a 21st-century version of cowboys. Whalen considers his role as the dying cowboy in Jeff Daniels' play *Panhandle Slim and The Oklahoma Kid* one of his most memorable, in part because of the tricks it required. "I wore a neoprene belt fitted with a supply of fake blood," he says. "During our premiere, by serendipity, the blood soaked through a hole in my shirt and mixed with the sawdust and dirt on the set. I definitely looked dead." He has faced death in three other plays—and in more rehearsals and performances than he can count.

Tom Whalen's introduction to theatrical life started when he was an altar boy. In On Golden Pond *(2012), he played the role of an aging professor.*

Although he has performed at theaters throughout the Midwest, he decided to center his career on the Purple Rose. "I feel very lucky to be where I am," he says. "I appreciate the care the people here devote to what they put on stage. The way they treat their personnel is unrivaled. I feel fortunate for the roles I've gotten on stage, and I feel equally fortunate to work with the apprentices. The Purple Rose has many strengths, but its biggest credential is the incredible apprenticeship program. Apprentices and actors here are set up to succeed." ■

Apprentice Molly Thomas with Michelle Mountain and Tom Whalen in The Glass Menagerie *(2005).*

PRTC
PRODUCTIONS

Bleeding Red 2009

Sea of Fools 2007

Boeing-Boeing 2010

Boom Town 1998

THE PURPLE ROSE *of* CHELSEA

PRTC
PRODUCTIONS

33 Variations 2013

The Mystery of Irma Vep 2004

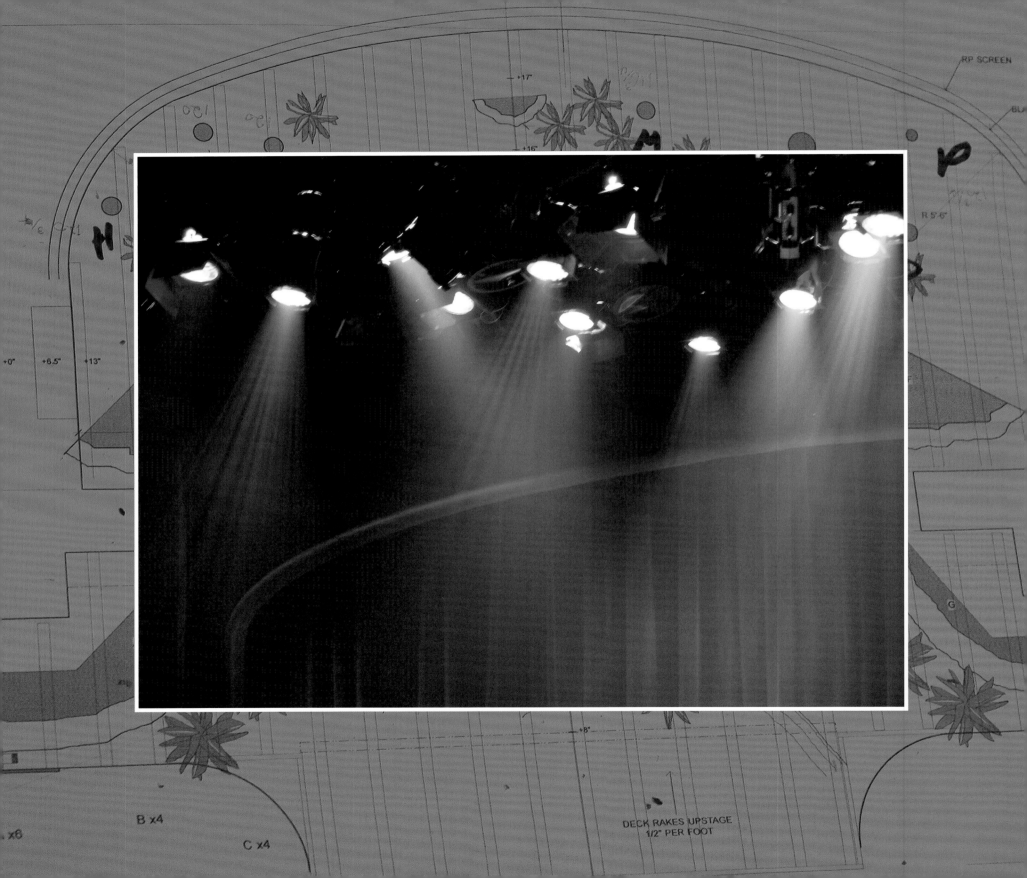

"We work very hard every day to give people the opportunity to do their best work. We want to spoil people, so they feel they've had one of the best work experiences of their lives." — GUY SANVILLE

CHAPTER 5

BEHIND THE SCENES

FIRST PRODUCTION MEETING, 2AZ, APRIL 16, 2015.

Squeezed around the conference table are Playwright/Actor Michael Brian Ogden, Literary Manager Michelle Mountain, Set Designer Gary Ciarkowski, Costume Designer Katherine Nelson, Properties Designer Danna Segrest, Sound Designer Tom Whalen, Managing Director Katie Doral, and Assistant Stage Manager Thomas Macias. With a coffee cup in one hand and a script in the other, Artistic Director Guy Sanville moves to the head of the table and Stage Manager Angie Kane Ferrante takes the foot. Three apprentices are perched on high stools in one corner of the room, poised to run, fetch, copy, and learn. Lighting and Projection Designer Noele Stollmack participates in the discussion via a Skype connection.

Sanville starts by reminding the group, "You all do a brilliant job, which is why you've been chosen. With a cast of sixteen, this is uncharted territory for us, which is very exciting. 2AZ is a project of distillation; our job is keeping it as elegant and powerful as possible."

He announces budgets: $7,000 for the set; $2,500 for props; $800 for set maintenance; $9,700 for costumes; $500 for the stitcher; $800 for costume maintenance; $800 for lights; $800 for sound; $1,000 for fake blood; $8,500 for projection equipment. "Angie, we also need a contract for Rob Najarian, the fight choreographer." Ferrante nods and jots a note.

"Now, the key word for this project is grit," the director says. "We'll see great firmness of character as these people continue on without complaint and with determination during a monumental disaster. Science fiction often serves as an allegory, so we know that this play isn't about zombies or an apocalypse, but about how humans respond to crises. We have tremendous things to explore in terms of key relationships. We'll have to trust our audience to imagine with us. At this point, I'm planning few scene changes and no black-outs, though that may change."

Stage Manager Angie Kane Ferrante leads actors in warm-up exercises before rehearsals and performances.

Production meetings introduce ideas from costume, lighting, set, properties, and sound designers. Lighting Designer Noele Stollmack, Sound Designer Tom Whalen, Assistant Stage Manager Thomas Macias, and Costume Designer Katherine Nelson meet with Guy Sanville.

"This is the story of grit: who has it and how it is manifested."

—GUY SANVILLE

He scans the people surrounding him and says, "In twenty-five words or less, what do you think this play is about?"

Michelle Mountain: "It's about a girl who has a choice to make and a secret mission that's revealed at the very end."

Gary Ciarkowski: "In the grander scheme, it's about society finding a reason to stay alive in the face of devastating circumstances."

Tom Whalen: "It's a version of Ulysses, an individual struggle to get home."

Angie Ferrante: "Life is a battle, and the characters struggle to figure out what life is really about and what the definition of 'survival' involves."

THE PURPLE ROSE *of* CHELSEA

"In *2AZ*, earth has decided to rid itself of the vermin called mankind. We want the idea of nature taking over." —GUY SANVILLE

Katie Doral: "This is a microcosm of society wondering if it's worth surviving, and if so, how to do it."

Danna Segrest: "I gravitate to the father-daughter dynamic. How do you protect each other when others don't feel they have a reason to survive?"

"I'm a conspiracy buff," Sanville says. "During the Kennedy and Martin Luther King assassinations, Americans became accustomed to news of atrocities. I was fifteen years old during the My Lai Massacre, watching Walter Cronkite show pictures of dead children shot by American soldiers; one looked to be the same age as my little sister. This group of Americans is dealing with that level of horror. On top of that, how do they respond when hot showers, hot food, homes, and safety go away? This is the story of grit: who has it and how it is manifested."

Ciarkowski discusses the set design, which will require the removal of the first row of theater seats and a projection screen at the rear of the stage.

When it's time to discuss lighting, Sanville waves moss-covered branches. "Noele," he tells the lighting designer, "there will be plant matter growing over everything. Earth has decided to rid itself of the vermin called mankind. We want the idea of nature taking over. That will be something for you to consider."

"My gut instinct is to be less realistic and more stylized. Like a *Twilight Zone* flashback," Stollmack suggests. Sanville nods.

Segrest pulls out (fake) body parts and (fake) blood. "Blood is made of different compounds, and some shouldn't be ingested," she reports. "I'm working on the consistency, so it won't shower the audience."

Katherine Nelson reports progress in distressing leather jackets with acetone, to age them. "Costumes will consist of layers, and each has a purpose: a belt so a knife can be strapped on it, jackets because it's cold," she says. "Clothing will be loose-fitting because these people are hungry and traumatized."

Sanville glances at his notes. "The two soldiers will be dressed in Marine Corps fatigues. Michelle, the U.S. president, should wear something official-looking, of a military character, and she should carry a sidearm. Angie, we should contact the actors and tell them to stop shaving and getting haircuts." Ferrante take notes.

Jeff Daniels shares thoughts and experiences before a performance.

Understudy actors listen intently to the first reading of 2AZ.

"I have a question about Kelly and Rachel," Mountain asks the playwright. "Are they similar or very different?"

"They're different, but they have things in common, and part of their journey is discovering that," Ogden says. "One is a nurse, a nurturer; the other is emotionally scarred, from a probable background of abuse. I think of them as being the same person, one ten years later."

Tom Whalen plays a medley of squishing, eerie, discordant sounds with vague voices in the background. "I immediately thought of Metallica when I read the script," he says. He follows that up with shorts from the album "Strange Trails" by the Michigan-based band Lord Huron.

"What about a Quentin Tarantino-type feel, something from "The Night We Met?" Sanville suggests. Whalen nods.

After precisely ninety minutes, Ferrante announces, "Next meeting is Friday the 24th. Two o'clock."

Four weeks of rehearsals will be followed by eight preview performances in which audiences will be asked for feedback. And then opening night.

FIRST READING, 2AZ. MAY 12, 2015.

By nine o'clock in the morning, the former Chelsea Center for the Arts hums, buzzes, and bangs with people and activities. Danna Segrest, properties manager, displays a staggering array of weapons arranged in order of their stage appearance. "I've been accumulating them for two years," she says. "These are real guns without the firing pins." Actors raise their eyebrows and look impressed. "Later," she promises, "we'll schedule lessons to teach you how to shoot."

Set designer Gary Ciarkowski stacks sections of the set. "This is a major project," he says. "We have a cast of sixteen, and occasionally they'll all be on stage at once, often fighting. That requires a much more rugged, substantial set than we usually build."

As nineteen people take seats at a very long table and eight understudies claim another nearby, Guy Sanville announces that Katherine Nelson will be taking measurements for costumes and Fight Choreographer Robert Najarian will conduct exercises to determine the actors' physical capabilites.

Scripts open, coffee cups full, Literary Manager Michelle Mountain says, "This is a second American Civil War, a zombie apocalypse, set in the future—but the not-too-distant future."

Sanville reminds the cast, "We're looking for powerful human reactions in the face of terrifying and imminent danger." He turns to the playwright. "Anything else we should know before we begin?"

"When the play opens, seventy percent of the world population has become zombies," Ogden says. "A small band of survivors will meet up with two members of a Delta Force after the 82nd Airborne has retaken Atlanta. The military's priority is to safeguard a vaccine and prioritize the population that will get the dosage. Among the survivors are two people of great interest to the government."

The Artistic Director supervises every aspect of the play through opening night, and then the stage manager takes over the show, preserving its integrity.

"I couldn't live without theater. I have a degree in performance, but directing and choreography is what I love. And the Purple Rose does theater the way I want to practice theater. They tell the truth." — ANGIE KANE FERRANTE

Assembling the stage requires help from everyone, apprentices especially.

Sanville reads stage directions as the reading proceeds. After two hours, "And…that's lunch!" he calls, as pizza boxes appear. By late afternoon, the reading ends. The costume designer, props manager, and fight choreographer begin their work.

"We have six weeks from the first day of rehearsal to the press opening," Sanville reminds his cast and crew.

Four weeks of rehearsals will be followed by eight preview performances in which audiences will be asked for feedback. And then opening night.

STAGE MANAGER

"Let's get in a circle and breathe," says Angie Kane Ferrante. "Breathe well….Breathe deep." As sixteen actors and eight understudies form a circle around her, the stage manager adds, "Now, let's do a ten-minute stretch." The actors arch their backs, reach for the ceiling, flop over at the waist, and stretch calf muscles as they roll their rrrrr's and produce an astonishing array of grunts, "aaaahhhh's," and "mmmmmm's".

"My mother was a music teacher who trained me well, and I'm a massage therapist, so I help Guy with the actors' physical preparations and vocalization work," Ferrante says. "Stage managers have to be flexible, focused, extremely detail-oriented, with an ability to see the big picture and to understand people. They have to put their personal feelings aside. And most of all, they have to juggle a dozen things at once."

A 2007 graduate of Wayne State's theater program, Ferrante studied at the Moscow Art Theatre in Russia. She ran a high school theater program for four years, then offered workshops in acting and directing before opening the AKT theatre company in Wyandotte. She met Guy Sanville when she won a spot in the PRTC Actor/Director Lab. He was impressed, and invited her to become a directing intern for *White Buffalo* in 2012.

"I couldn't live without theater," Ferrante says. "I have a degree in performance, but directing and choreography is what I love. And the Purple Rose does theater the way I want to practice theater. They tell the truth. That seems really simple, but it's crucial to the success of a play."

On opening night for Talley's Folly, Director
Angie Kane Ferrante poses with Robert Najarian
and Aphrodite Nikolovski. This was Ferrante's
first directing job at the PRTC.

A master at multi-tasking, she orchestrates pre-production meetings with the efficiency and aptitude of the best corporate CEOs—not an easy task when dealing with as many as two dozen professionals at once. She works closely with the director throughout rehearsals and previews, taking copious notes and making sure all aspects of the production are on task and on time. After opening night, she takes Sanville's place as supervisor; then the job focuses on maintaining the quality, integrity, and million small details that make a production run smoothly.

When her PRTC directing internship ended, Ferrante stage managed *Redwood Curtain*, *The Vast Difference*, *Miles and Ellie*, *Annapurna*, *Steel Magnolias*, *2AZ*, and *Casting Session*, which, she says, presented enormous challenges because of the size of the cast (sixteen), the many

Ogden's play 2AZ presented
new challenges, ranging from
zombies to a cast of sixteen.

"Stage managers have
to be on their toes at
all times."

—ANGIE KANE FERRANTE

choreographed fight scenes, the amount of (fake) blood that was shed, and the complexity of the play. For the anniversary season, she was selected to stage manage *Casting Session, The Odd Couple*, and *Morning's At Seven.*

Ferrante credits Stephanie Buck with invaluable advice about stage management: "Your biggest challenge is keeping your mouth shut. Stage managers are not supposed to give their artistic ideas. Their job is to support and carry out the visions of the playwright, director, designers, and, ultimately, Jeff Daniels."

"Stage managers have to be on their toes at all times, and they must keep learning," Ferrante says. "I take classes. I learn everything I can from Guy. Things change constantly in this business—that's the nature of the theater."

Ferrante designed the sound for *Steel Magnolias* and *Casting Session*, and her first chance at directing a PRTC performance, *Talley's Folly*, became a career milestone, she says. "Directing was everything I dreamed it would be. Ultimately, directing is what I want to do."

Reviewers endorse that idea. Jenn McKee, of MLive.com called *Talley's Folly* "a 35-year-old valentine that retains its charm," and John Quinn noted, "While the play, indeed, progresses with the grace and gentility of a waltz, director Angie Kane Ferrante's sprightly interpretation renders "Folley" as brisk as a quick-step."

ONE REVIEW CALLED *TALLEY'S FOLLY* "A 35-YEAR-OLD VALENTINE THAT RETAINS ITS CHARM."

Talley's Folly 2015

*Technical Director
Gary Ciarkowski supervises
a team of apprentices
during the construction and
installation of sets.*

Set Design

SET DESIGN

Gary Ciarkowski

On a blistering hot day, Technical Director Gary Ciarkowski and apprentice Mikey Wecht are pounding nails into two-by-fours in the parking lot outside the design shop. "This is only the third set I've designed," Ciarkowski says, showing his plans for 2AZ. "Normally I just build them."

In his job, timing is tight and essential—and so is the space in which he works, which is why sets often spill into the parking lot. The minute one show closes, the set is struck and a new set installed, requiring three fourteen-hour days and a twenty-foot dumpster. "It's a challenge to get everything done on time," he says.

Ciarkowski came to the Purple Rose through the back door—literally. "My Dad was a carpenter and I've always built stuff, but my degree is in aerospace engineering," the University

"I always knew that if something broke, Gary could fix it." — DAPHNE HODDER

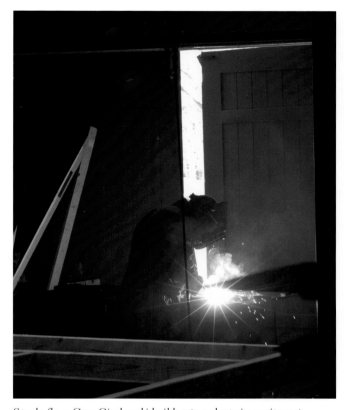

Sparks fly as Gary Ciarkowski builds sets and repairs equipment.

of Michigan alumnus says. His five-year work-study job put him in the lighting and sound department for the university's Musical Society, which is where PRTC Technical Director Dan Walker found him in 1996, when he needed a master electrician with experience in productions. For several years Ciarkowski juggled theater work with his full-time job at the Alternate Lighting Company before hiring on full-time when Walker left.

Like many jobs behind the scenes, his requires monumental multi-tasking. Former Box Office Manager Daphne Hodder recalls, "I always knew that if something broke, Gary could fix it." When a lighting or sound catastrophe occurs during rehearsals or performances, Ciarkowski is called. "Fortunately for us, Gary lives nearby," Ferrante says. When he's not building sets or answering distress calls, he supervises building maintenance and lighting placement.

Each set design brings its own challenges, he says. "My primary considerations are the numbers of people in the show and the best way the set can help tell the story." He reads the script, listens to the actors' readings, and discusses ideas with Sanville before putting pencil to paper.

Although 2AZ presented major challenges because of its large cast and fight scenes, Ciarkowski remembers the set of *Boeing-Boeing* as particularly difficult because it was a luxurious apartment requiring drywall, elaborate decorating, and extensive electrical work. "But each set poses new challenges," he says. For Vince Mountain's *Redwood Curtain* design, he built trees. *Talley's Folly* required the illusion of a river, which he accomplished with a mixture of paint and a particularly hard resin used for bar tops. The effect was dramatic and realistic.

Set builders and designers suffer their share of catastrophes. Perhaps the worst happened when the sprinkler system drenched the set of *Months on End*, Ciarkowski recalls. Every apprentice was commandeered to mop the floors and dry the staging.

"For years, we used volunteers from the community, but no longer," he adds, nodding at his apprentice. "You have to keep volunteers happy. You have to treat them with kid gloves. You can't berate them. Apprentices, on the other hand, have to listen to me and do what I say."

In an Oscar-worthy performance, Mikey Wecht groans and rolls his eyes.

"Everything I put on the stage has to have a purpose and make a statement."

— BARTLEY H. BAUER

Bartley Bauer won the Detroit News Theatre Award *for best design for his* Blithe Spirit *set.*

Escanaba in da Moonlight *required construction of a log cabin with front porch—which meant teaching cabin-building skills to apprentices.*

Bartley H. Bauer

"The design process here is much more interactive than at most other theaters," Bartley Bauer says. "I sit down with the artistic director, costume designer, lighting designer, stage manager, and assistants, and we share ideas. We create together. That doesn't happen everywhere."

He reads the script repeatedly before determining the "needs, wants, and desires (based on budget)." And then he begins weeding out ideas. "If Guy is the director, we spend a lot of time talking," Bauer says. "My job is to support his interpretation of the script. He spends months preparing ideas."

Bauer calls his sets "lean." "Everything I put on the stage has to have a purpose and make a statement. A lantern in a corner will say something important about the time and style. One set I designed consisted of just one couch."

Ciarkowski builds the sets, then Bauer finishes them, painting and coordinating decorating with Properties Manager Danna Segrest. "That's the fun part," he says. His favorite sets include a Quonset hut on stilts; a cemetery where people rose from, and returned to, graves; a boathouse; and a trailer half-sunk in a swamp. "I particularly like abstract things, as well as the fun, crazy stuff."

Like Jeff Daniels, Bauer began his theatrical career in Chelsea, with music teacher DiAnn L'Roy, as part of the Chelsea Area Players Jr. Then he earned degrees in theater arts management. His full-time job is designing baths and kitchens for Chelsea Lumber; nights and weekends, he designs sets, including more than twenty PRTC sets over its quarter-century history.

Bartley Bauer says his greatest sense of pride comes from watching apprentices like Julia Garlotte grow in their skills and move on to other theaters.

Set Designer Bart Bauer and Lighting Designer Dana White work together frequently.

The staging for *Annapurna* won Bauer the 2015 Wilde Award for set design and *Blithe Spirit* received the *Detroit News* Theatre Award for Best Design. "I always find that if the actors do a really good job, no one mentions the set. That's the sign that we have all done our part well," Bauer says.

Vince Mountain

A boy who loved to build card-stock models grew into a professor who loves to build and design scenery for theater, opera, and film. After earning a B.A. degree in theater from Penn State University and an M.F.A. in design from UC/San Diego, Vince Mountain became professor of scenic design at the University of Michigan. In academia, professors in the arts are expected to maintain creative activities off campus as the equivalent of publishing. Mountain has designed sets at regional theaters across the country, as well as twenty-two PRTC sets (the twenty-third will be 2016's *Gaps in the Fossil Record*). He has been a Resident Artist since 1996.

He also designed sets for ABC Network's *Detroit 1-8-7* and Paramount Pictures' *Transformers IV* and *Looking for Alaska*. "Designing sets for theater and for films requires similar skills, but otherwise there is a big difference," he says. "Movies and television are often based on realism. In the theater, a barn is built of Styrofoam and painted to look like wood. What I like about theater is the great variety of possibilities, where the physical environment can be expressed more suggestively and the set can be more abstract. Every play offers the chance to create a new world that only exists for a particular play."

He says that all plays are a challenge to envision at first. "A writer faces the proverbial two-dimensional blank page, but a set designer has to face an empty stage in three dimensions. I always start out telling myself, 'I don't know what to do.' Ultimately, the set develops, not based strictly on my aesthetic, but on the best way to serve the play and bring the world to life."

Jenn McKee of MLive reviewed the 2014 regional theater highlights and noted, "One of the undeniable stars of the Purple Rose Theatre's *Redwood Curtain* was Vincent Mountain's lush forest, beautifully lit by Noele Stollmack. It was a haunting, gorgeous wonder."

COSTUME DESIGN

Suzanne Young

"Stand up," Guy Sanville asks Michelle Mountain during an apprentice workshop. She does. He turns to his apprentices and says, "Look very closely. She is in great shape physically. She has great hair, a long torso, shoulders like a linebacker. When we dress her, all those attributes come into play. Costume designers exploit some of them and hide others, depending on the role."

Suzanne Young is one of those costume designers. Growing up in England, she watched her mother and friends perform Shakespeare in a National Trust garden every summer. Then,

when she was eight, she began helping them choose costumes. "I was completely awed by the world of period dress. It's a marvelous form of escapism," she says. "This is a passion, an abiding interest for me. Costume design is in my blood."

In the early 1980s, Young studied costuming at the Wimbledon School of Art and Design in London and dressed the BBC's Shakespearean actors, opera and ballet stars. Later, she ran the wardrobe department for the Opera Company of Boston before establishing her own business, American Costume Design. After a sojourn in France, her family moved to Ann Arbor, and in 2011, she was asked to design the costumes for *Escanaba in da Moonlight*, followed by *33 Variations*; *The PRTC Spring Comedy Festival: Lovers, Liars, & Lunatics*; *Annapurna*; and *Morning's At Seven*. Her work won the 2014 Wilde Award for Costume Design.

"They were all wonderful experiences, but *33 Variations* was especially great fun because it required modern and period dress," she says. "I'm looking forward to *Morning's At Seven* because it's set in the 1930s and involves at least seven characters."

Young's library includes two hundred costume books as well as online resources. "I love doing the research," she says. She attends production meetings to discuss her ideas about originality, colors, and period; then she sets to work with pencil and paper. Throughout the design process, she works closely with Sanville, who watches the fittings and gives feedback, occasionally suggesting changes. She is one of the few designers who can—and sometimes will—do the sewing.

Christianne Myers has to be part psychiatrist for the characters she clothes.

Lighting

> "I usually fall in love with everything I'm working on at the time. I tell my students I have to know why I choose to do a play—and 'the paycheck' is not an acceptable answer." — CHRISTIANNE MYERS

The setting, season, characters' socioeconomic background, and actions within the play suggest costume ideas, she says. And then research and imagination take over. "I work with the director's vision and give it my own interpretation." She provides clothing and hats, and relies on Danna Segrest for accessories.

Christianne Myers

"I was a backstage baby," Christianne Myers says. "Both of my parents were in performing arts, so, naturally, I was a theater geek. I had no desire to be on stage, though. I liked design, particularly costume design."

She interned at the Circle Repertory Theatre when Jeff Daniels was starring in Lanford Wilson's *Redwood Curtain*. After earning a master's degree from New York University, she joined the University of Michigan faculty and met Vince Mountain, who introduced her to Guy Sanville in 2002.

Myers created period costumes for Isaac Newton and the cast of *Gravity*; four outfits each for the six ladies in *Steel Magnolias*; and wardrobes for the iconic *A Streetcar Named Desire*. Period costumes are easier to design, she says, because "everyone is an expert on contemporary dress, although it varies widely, depending on the character's age, status, nationality, taste, region, and season. I have to be part psychiatrist to choose appropriate outfits."

She works closely with the set designer and properties manager, to make sure she dresses a character to coordinate with her environment. "Will Danna put *Good Housekeeping* or *Architectural Digest* on the coffee table? That will make a decision in the type of costume," she says.

"I usually fall in love with everything I'm working on at the time. I tell my students I have to know why I choose to do a play—and 'the paycheck' is not an acceptable answer."

LIGHTING

Dana White

"This is an embarrassing story," Dana White warns, grinning.

"In 1991, there was a rush to finish the set for the first show, *Blush at Nothing*, so a friend asked me to help paint. Everyone was hard at work in the Garage Theater when a newcomer joined us. He asked me what I did for a living."

White told him he'd finished a master's degree in theater lighting. Then he asked, "What do you do?"

"My name is Jeff, and this is my theater," the newcomer said.

"I felt about two inches tall," White admitted, laughing. But that night Jeff Daniels told him the theater could use a lighting designer. Less than a month later, White was hired. "I've lost count of how many shows I've worked on. Forty? Forty-two?" he says.

He teaches in Ohio and commutes to Chelsea. Like all designers, he has his own style. "I understand that actors hear character voices in their heads. I don't, but I usually have a complete image of what the play looks like in my head—as if there's a movie running in there. It's more along the lines of mapping visions."

A musician, White met world-famous lighting designers during his concerts. Thanks to them, his own light bulb went on. He grew so fascinated by the art of lighting that he decided to learn more. As a graduate student, he read an article in *American Theater Magazine* discussing how Marshall Mason worked with his lighting designer. White told himself, "I'll know that I've made it when I can do lighting for an original version of a Lanford Wilson play." His dream came true at the Purple Rose, when he worked on *Book of Days*.

"I was just a kid from the Midwest, but I knew I was playing in the big leagues then," he says. "I feel tremendously privileged to have worked with Lanford. He inspired me to look deeply, to use lighting in subtle and in-depth ways. I separate my professional life into two parts: before and after *Book of Days*."

Typically, White's style offers contrast and abundant but subtle color, although some scripts demand an aggressive, more obvious style. The 2015 production of Wilson's *Talley's Folly* offered special challenges: "It was almost one long light cue," he explains. "We had between thirty-five and forty cues, some of them three or four minutes long. *Casting Session*,

Like all designers, Dana White has his own style.

During rehearsals, lighting designers study the sets, characters' skin tones, costumes, and elements of drama when they create lighting blueprints. Then apprentices help run cables, even through the ceilings.

on the other hand, required twenty-five cues over seventy minutes. Because *Book of Days* was episodic in nature, 160 cues were needed, some of them only two seconds in duration."

White's process starts with a careful study of the script, to understand the story and its environment: Warm and comfortable? Isolated and cold? Early morning, high noon, dusk, or evening? "I go first for emotional content much the same way a novelist works," he says. He breaks the script down into shifts, identifying characters' power shifts or the points at which crucial pieces of information are revealed. Then he meets with the director, sometimes bringing photos to demonstrate his vision for evoking visceral feelings.

During rehearsals, he studies actors' skin tones, costume fabrics, and set materials before mapping out his lighting design, which will be refined and edited during the first reading and again during the technical rehearsal and after previews.

"This is a dynamic, collaborative process," he says. "The Purple Rose expects it to be done right. We're all given a lot of free rein to do our very best. Working with Lanford was a terrific exposure to that level of excellence. I still see his influence at the Purple Rose."

Reid Johnson

Reid Johnson's involvement with the Purple Rose parallels Dana White's. Twenty-five years ago, Johnson tagged along with a friend doing the lighting for *Weekend Comedy*. Jeff Daniels asked Johnson about his credentials (a bachelor's degree in scenic design and a master's in lighting from the Hilberry Theatre) and hired him shortly afterwards. Johnson has worked on twenty-four PRTC shows.

"My job is to focus the audience's attention on the actors and action, not on the lighting," he says. "To help tell the story, we sometimes design lighting to see the actor, and other times to showcase the environment, or reveal the weather or time of day."

While studying the script, he identifies places where moods change. Dramas tend to be darker than comedies, for instance. It's essential that back-row audience members must be able to see everything. Lighting also reveals setting (Indoors? Outdoors?) and time of day. During pre-production meetings, Johnson studies the set design, then, he says, the read-through brings his ideas to life.

"Some directors know specifically what they want the lighting to accomplish. Some don't have a big vocabulary in lighting, but know what they like when they see it. And some leave the interpretation to me," he says. "Guy is very knowledgeable and stays close throughout the technical rehearsal. He'll frequently say, 'Try this.' It's great to have strong direction and feedback."

During rehearsals, Johnson studies the ways actors use the space, then draws a blueprint detailing lights' placement for Master Electrician Gary Ciarkowski and his apprentices. During the technical rehearsal, the lighting plan is tested, revised, and recorded as Reid Johnson sits with the apprentices at the light board. He attends at least three more rehearsals, to fine-tune

the plan. Later, audiences' comments after the previews may result in additional changes. Once everything is set in stone—or, rather, computer—the apprentices manage the lighting duties.

Across the Way presented one of Johnson's greatest challenges, he recalls, because of the number of small scenes between two or three people on a big, open stage. *Panhandle Slim & The Oklahoma Kid* required the illusion of brilliant sunlight in a colorful desert. Set in an old cabin, *Escanaba In Love* needed lighting to suggest a wintery U. P. outside the windows. *Let It Be* took place in a hotel room inhabited by different guests. "Some changes were brilliant," he says. "When the maid came in to clean, we used very neutral lighting, then lighting changed to reflect the feel of the room when it was inhabited by different people."

"I love the Purple Rose intimacy," Johnson says. "The small size is beautiful for doing intimate work. That thrust stage makes the action feel as if it's taking place within the audience."

"I love the Purple Rose intimacy. The small size is beautiful for doing intimate work."

—REID JOHNSON

Jack-of-all trades Danna Segrest captures the pre-production process on film.

Sound Design

"Sound designers read scripts like a detective, searching for specific clues about the action that will take place on stage." — TOM WHALEN

SOUND DESIGN

Tom Whalen

"I like the challenge of becoming proficient in whatever new thing I do, which is how I got into sound design," actor/singer/sound technician Tom Whalen says. He was responsible for the sounds in *Apartment 3A, Consider the Oyster, A Street Car Named Desire, On Golden Pond, Annapurna, The Last Romance, Talley's Folly,* and *2AZ.*

Sound designers are not only responsible for pre- and post-performance music, but also for doors slamming, shots firing, whistles blowing, phones ringing, corks popping, trees rustling, winds howling, and fight sounds, all on cue.

Whalen's interest in sound production dates back to his teenage years. "I played in rock 'n' roll bands—everyone did in the Sixties and Seventies, and I took lessons on the viola, stand-up bass, sax, and trumpet. I won't say I'm versatile, but I can be cast in plays that require instruments." For PRTC roles, he learned to play the mandolin and ukulele.

"Sound designers read scripts like a detective, searching for specific clues about the action that will take place on stage," he says. Then he sets to work, listening to CDs, YouTube recordings, and the materials in the theater's library. His job requires close coordination of sounds with the lighting, set, actions on stage, and the director. "There's nothing worse than a delayed *Bang!* after a gun is fired or a door is slammed," he points out.

Whalen often reviews his work with Resident Artist Dan Bilich, a gifted local musician who has taken acting classes at the theater. "He plays several instruments and has a good ear for what works," Whalen says. He also works closely with the apprentices, requiring each one to write a "bible" for sound technicians ("starting with where the ON button can be found") before they "graduate" to another aspect of their training. "Our job is to make these kids ready for all the work in any theater," he says. "I'm impressed and awed with the type of talent our apprenticeship program brings in. I couldn't do my job without them."

THE PURPLE ROSE *of* CHELSEA

Left: Blood may be thicker than water, but Danna Segrest's fake blood is thicker than chocolate sauce.

Below: Escanaba *props were Danna Segrest's responsibility for the plays as well as the film* Escanaba in da Moonlight.

PROPERTIES DESIGN

Danna Segrest

Danna Segrest is experimenting with the consistency of blood by mixing chocolate, corn syrup, and red food coloring. "Too thick and it turns into a disgusting gravy, too thin and it'll spray the audience," she explains, adding, "Guy dubbed me 'the pro with blood.' We've used it many times, often with Tom Whalen as the dead or dying guy." Once she perfects the consistency, her next challenge is to determine how to hide a baggie of the stuff on Whalen's body so he can burst it surreptitiously during his 2AZ death scene. "There's never a dull moment in my job," Segrest adds.

Her history with the Purple Rose goes back to the dark ages—literally—when the Garage Theater was under renovation and the first PRTC auditions were held in the Chelsea Methodist Church. A Michigan State graduate who studied theater and communications, she apprenticed at Northville's Marquis Theater, then took a public relations job while moonlighting on theater productions. In 1990, when she heard rumors about Jeff Daniels' theater plans, she immediately contacted Doug Beaumont and Bart Bauer, offering to help in any way. "Help in any way" became the motto of her twenty-five-year association with the PRTC.

"I love, love, love this job. There is always something interesting to learn for every play." — DANNA SEGREST

In the early days, she took care of everything from light bulbs to office supplies, mailings, tickets, and props. She supervised apprentices while working as assistant stage manager for *Shoe Man*, earning her Actors Equity card and served as "overlap stage manager" when one show ran into its successor's rehearsal schedule. Nowadays she works part-time in the box office; maintains theater archives; takes photos; collects, stores, and distributes props; works on sets; accessorizes costumes; and coaches actors on the use of everything from blood bags to guns.

"Some plays come with a published list of props, but if we're doing a world premiere, I create the list of props and furnishings needed for the set," Segrest says. She brainstorms with the director, set designers, and costume designers, then lists needs and identifies sources.

"We try to borrow as much as possible because we have no storage space and a low budget," she explains. "A lot can happen to portable items during the run of a play, so I keep close track of everything."

Although she says that every show is "cool in its own way," some create theater legends. She recalls the energy on the set of *The Tropical Pickle* when Guy Sanville first appeared on

stage; the potential disaster when Michael Brian Ogden's character broke his leg and needed a cast during *Consider the Oyster;* the night the sprinkler system drenched the *Months on End* stage; and the excitement of watching Jeff Daniels write the *Escanaba in da Moonlight* trilogy—backwards, the way Lanford Wilson wrote.

As properties manager for the *Escanaba in da Moonlight* movie, she had to transport all the props to the Upper Peninsula in winter. When cameras started rolling, three feet of snow covered the ground; as it melted during the filming, Danna and assistants had to shovel snow back onto the set. During *Gravity*, a pot was broken during every performance and Segrest had to supply new ones; she talked a local potter into making seventy-seven versions of the same vessel. 33 *Variations* required an entire library. She supplied Guy Sanville with fresh cream puffs during every performance of *Sea of Fools.*

"I love, love, love this job," Segrest says. "There is always something interesting to learn for every play." She toured a funeral parlor for *Wake*, become an expert in baseball cards for *Honus and Me*, and taught gun safety and the use of high-powered weaponry for *2AZ*. "We learned that firing blanks is too hard on the ears in this theater," she says. "The way it echoes sounds wrong to the audience. Tom Whalen had a big job to design all the sounds for that show." Segrest had an equally challenging job accumulating the weaponry to produce those sounds. Her behind-the-scenes work has not gone unnoticed. She won the 2015 Wilde Award for her work on *Annapurna*. ■

Blithe Spirit 2003

Gravity 2010

THE PURPLE ROSE *of* CHELSEA

PRTC
PRODUCTIONS

Nooner 1993

2AZ 2015

"The apprenticeship program was intended to give back to others, to teach…kids what they need to know about this business. It's not easy work. Apprentices get experience in all aspects of theater—onstage and behind the scenes." —JEFF DANIELS

Danna Segrest catches Stephanie Buck leading Stage Makeup class with Apprentices Kelly Vieau, Jessica Garrett, and Josh Roth.

Education is taken very seriously at the Purple Rose. Since its founding, the theater has offered classes in acting, directing, and movement; actors' boot camps; Shakespeare; acting intensives for teens; playwriting intensives; play readings in libraries and for civic organizations; and an apprenticeship program that promises to become "an experience like no other."

"They mean that," former Apprentice Lauren Knox says.

"We're here to introduce our community to the arts in many ways," Guy Sanville says. "But the apprenticeship program is the jewel in our crown."

"There is truly nothing like our apprenticeship program anywhere else," Managing Director and former Apprentice Katie Doral agrees. "Most apprenticeships are specific to one aspect of theater. We've created a program that develops apprentices into well-rounded professionals who know and understand all aspects of the theater. Apprentices train in both the business and creative end of the theater, and they end their apprenticeship with Dark Night, the equivalent of a thesis. They write, direct, produce, design, stage manage, market, and act in an evening of short plays."

The PRTC hires seven apprentices each season. Over the course of thirteen months, they work between fifty-eight and seventy-four hours each week doing everything. They clean toilets, build sets, shovel snow, hang lights, crew shows, take classes, sell tickets, write, direct, and act. "They are the backbone of the theater," Apprentice Chief Michelle Mountain says. "They are constantly learning."

THE EDUCATION

Matthew Gwynn and Nate Mitchel share a scene in a reading at the Ann Arbor Public Library.

Because the PRTC produces four shows each year, each apprentice holds seven or eight different crew positions, including working in the shop and box office; serving as house manager and working with props; operating the sound board and maintaining the costumes; assisting the master electrician, serving as light board operator, maintaining the set; serving as production assistant to the stage manager and the backstage crew; maintaining the props; and rotating as rehearsal assistant and crew backup. "They leave here knowing how a small professional theater operates from the ground up," Mountain says.

The apprentices also have the opportunity to participate in the script review process; audition; learn at the right hand of experts in theater-related disciplines; participate in classes and workshops; and attend table readings, rehearsals, and production meetings. "Our goal is to offer apprentices experience in all aspects of the business of running a small nonprofit," Jeff Daniels says. "We originally modeled the program after the Circle Rep apprentice program, but over the years it has become much, much better."

Because the work schedule is so demanding, apprentices are not permitted to hold outside jobs, so the theater offers a stipend to cover housing and living expenses. Apprentices can apply for equity membership candidacy and earn points toward their equity card, either as a production/rehearsal assistant to the stage manager or by acting in, or understudying for, a main stage production.

Apprentices work on the Human Machine exercise.

Apprentice Chief Michelle Mountain appeared in
33 Variations (2013).

"There are a lot of doors here waiting to be opened," Mountain tells newcomers. "Your drive, initiative, and ambition are the keys to opening them. Be prepared for hard work and a steep learning curve. You have an opportunity here to do better than your best, and to leave here knowing you can do anything you set your heart and mind to. And, as an important bonus, you'll make life-long friends."

"The apprenticeship program benefits all of us—apprentices, actors, designers, and administrators," says actor Rhiannon Ragland. "The Purple Rose has an amazing training system, designed so the apprentices have our backs at all times….Because they take the worry and production details away, they allow actors to do our best jobs. We commit ourselves to one-hundred-percent effort, to show our respect for their hard work. Apprentices make our days easier. It's an amazing privilege to work with them."

"The apprentices work their butts off," agrees Stage Manager Angie Kane Ferrante. "As assistant stage managers, they physically hand each actor their props and take them from them when they exit the stage. They're responsible for giving them water or towels or whatever else they need. And that's just the start."

The majority of apprentices hail from the Midwest, although applications come from across the nation and around the world. The first 139 apprentices clocked more than five thousand service hours in the arts.

"I was thirty before I truly understood how to act. I had to watch lots of people to understand the difference between pretending and performing. When you're performing, you're thinking, reacting, and responding to the world as the character would." —STEPHANIE BUCK

Guy Sanville with Apprentices Nicole Bartell and Julie Brunzell.

"I think the Purple Rose has a sixth sense for selecting ideal young people. Every one I've met has been totally trustworthy, hardworking, and dedicated to the good of the entire company," says Costume Designer Christianne Myers. "The apprenticeship program is the backbone of the Purple Rose. It's an outstanding mentorship program for young people interested in every aspect of the theater. The apprentices provide helping hands and hard work for the staff."

She calls its protocol "elegant," one she hasn't seen elsewhere. "Here, the response to anything is 'Thank you'," Myers says. "That sounds so small, but it acknowledges your work and it acknowledges that you've been heard. I don't see that kind of courtesy in any other theater."

"At the end of the apprenticeship, they will know what they need to do to become an actor, director, stage manager, lighting designer, sound designer, or set designer in New York," Daniels says. "We emphasize reliability, professionalism, responsibility, and teamwork."

When Bart Bauer is asked to choose the set design that makes him proudest, he declines. "It's not one set, but all the people I've been able to get to know." he says. "I'm proud to play even a small part in their careers. The amount of local talent we've developed is, in my opinion, our company's biggest achievement."

Former PRTC apprentices work in many regional and national theaters. Tony Casselli runs the Williamston Theater. James Kuhl is artistic director of the Tipping Point Theatre, and most of his staff apprenticed at the Purple Rose. Aaron Rossini is the co-artistic director of the Fault Line Theatre, and Joseph Reecher is a lighting supervisor and IT analyst at the Public Theatre, both in New York City. Molly Thomas performs with the Upright Citizen's Brigade. Joseph Zettelmaier has written two dozen plays that have been produced professionally. Lynn Lammers and Stefanie Din both hold teaching positions at Michigan State University. Others work on and off Broadway and in Chicago, while some have used their training in very different professions.

2015 Apprentice Class:
Jowi Estava, Colleen Miner, Jillian Joie Clements ,
Julia Cassell, Megan Pinto, Mikey Wecht, Erika Thiede.

THE APPRENTICES

Stephanie Buck

When Stephanie Buck is asked to choose words to describe the Purple Rose, she instantly says, "Home. Beginning. Magic."

Yet she intended to become a lawyer when she enrolled at Central Michigan University. She majored in theater, telling herself that the skills would come in handy in a courtroom, but she changed career direction after enrolling in a PRTC voice and movement class at the urging of her mother, a member of the Saline Area Players. Michelle Mountain convinced Buck to become an apprentice. In 2007, when her year ended, Guy Sanville invited her to remain as stage manager.

"Stage managers don't get recognition, but it's a great way to support yourself," Buck says. "I like taking care of people, being the facilitator for a successful show. The stage manager's goal is to take away everyone's worries, help them forget the details, and allow them to focus on their jobs."

Buck had the opportunity to direct *Redwood Curtain*, which she considers her greatest achievement, although she enjoyed transforming into a zombie for her husband's play, 2AZ. "I was thirty before I truly understood how to act. I had to watch lots of people to understand

Stephanie Buck considers the opportunity to direct
Redwood Curtain *her greatest professional acheivement.*

Apprentice spoof of
The Subject was Roses:
Julia Garlotte, Jessica Garrett,
Rick Eva, Stephanie Buck,
Matthew Gwynn, Nathan Oliver,
Wesley Speary, Jeffery Hannah.

the difference between pretending and performing," she says. "When you're performing, you're thinking, reacting, and responding to the world as the character would. You're not informing the audience of your thoughts."

The Purple Rose made her more courageous in exploring her voice and craft, she says. "The biggest lesson I learned here was never to hold back. The Purple Rose challenged us to take a leap, give everything a try, and stop editing yourself before you try something."

"Running the business is not the glamorous side of the theater, but I'm thrilled that I can help the place that has made me who I am." —KATIE DORAL

Buck and her husband Michael Brian Ogden took those lessons to heart. They moved to New York City when 2AZ closed. "The Purple Rose has taught us that you can have art anywhere. You don't need to move to New York to create something that moves people, but we're young and confident and ready to try our luck. That's part of the adventure," Buck says.

Katie Doral

Katie Doral first met Guy, Michelle, and Jeff Daniels when they taught a theater arts class at Albion College in 1998, when she was a freshman. "It was emotionally draining, but such an incredible class," she says. "I never forgot what Jeff Daniels taught us: 'It's not really about where you go to school as much as being in the right place at the right time, ready to say 'yes'." And, she adds, Daniels also told her, "It's the people you meet who will guide you on your way."

"I'm living proof of that," she says.

She began acting in children's plays at the age of four. In high school she segued from acting to directing, and by her junior and senior year she was directing her own work and serving as assistant director for the plays at her school, as well as in her community. After graduating from Albion, she enrolled in the apprenticeship program. "Purple Rose professionals showed me that I could make a career doing what I loved to do," she says.

In 2002, when her apprenticeship ended, the PRTC hired her as a union assistant stage manager, then the alpha stage manager. Four years later, she left for Milwaukee, eventually becoming general manager of First Stage Children's Theater. "I had incredible mentors, both at the Purple Rose and in Milwaukee," she says. "I was able to learn so much here and take it somewhere else." In 2013, she returned to the PRTC as managing director.

"I still love directing and stage managing, but I absolutely love the managing director role. Running the business is not the glamorous side of the theater, but I'm thrilled that I can help the place that has made me who I am."

Managing Director Katie Doral will soon supervise a major facilities expansion that will include a larger lobby, classrooms, and rehearsal space.

Guy Sanville and Michelle Moutain shared the stage in Born Yesterday *(2002).*

Lauren Knox, pictured here with Michelle Mountain and Michael Brian Ogden, landed her roll in 33 Variations *while still in her apprentice year.*

Lauren Knox

"Guy told us that half the battle is showing up. By the very nature of being here, my life was enriched," Lauren Knox says "During the apprenticeship, everyone has to be willing to do the job no one else wants to do—without taking the credit for the success."

Her professional rise was meteoric. While still an apprentice—and while continuing all her apprentice duties—she appeared in one play and understudied for another, quickly earning her equity card. After completing her apprenticeship, she went on to understudy in *Redwood Curtain*, perform in *The Spring Comedy Festival*, serve as directing intern for *Annapurna*, and perform in *Steel Magnolias* and *2AZ*. In the twenty-fifth season, she will direct Guy Sanville in *The Odd Couple*, and she assists Michelle Mountain with the summer teen intensive.

"I am so thankful to Jeff Daniels for giving us the opportunity to do good work without moving to L.A.," she says. "Here was everything I wanted: the chance to act, direct, and have a family. Guy taught us that the key to happiness is passion, and he stressed that we can have what we want, if we work towards it."

But the theater requires sacrifices, she admits. "When you work in the theater, you have to be prepared to miss holidays, parties, and weddings. And sometimes the work has an emotional cost as well." But she is willing to make the sacrifices, she says. In spare moments, she does voice-overs for radio and television.

"The universe has a funny way of putting you where you need to grow."

— THOMAS MACIAS

2014 Apprentice Class: Owen Likley, Thomas Macias, John Forgrave, Nathan Magyar, April Warner, Devan Malone, and Adair Whalen.

"During my apprenticeship, I grew so much, as a professional in the theater world and as a person. I learned about myself and how to communicate with others. Michelle Mountain told us, *Excellence is a habit. You are what you repeatedly do. Aim to do a little more than your best every day.* That's great advice for everyone. The Purple Rose taught us to be in a constant learning mode, to develop the integrity to do our best work whether or not someone was watching."

Thomas Macias

"The universe has a funny way of putting you where you need to grow," says Thomas Macias, a 2014 apprentice who was born in Hawaii and graduated from Rochester (N.Y.) Institute of Technology. "My father is deaf, my mother is a sign language interpreter, and my family is Hispanic, all of which gave me a strong appreciation for self-expression in a wide variety of forms." Among his early career highlights was the chance to offer his voice for a signed performance of *Guys and Dolls*. "I moved in sync with the signer," he explains. "That was an entirely new challenge for me."

Thomas Macias will stage manage the 2016 production of Gaps in the Fossil Record.

33 *Variations* introduced him to theater the way PRTC does theater. As an apprentice, he especially enjoyed his rotations in stage management and the box office, he says. "The apprenticeship was the hardest year of my life. I grew tremendously—but I didn't see that happening because I was so exhausted and so consumed by all that I was doing and learning."

The PRTC hired Thomas as a stage management intern when his apprenticeship ended. He earned his equity card during the rehearsals of *Steel Magnolias*. After many positions as assistant, he will stage manage *Gaps in the Fossil Record*. "I'm excited and nervous," he says, "but I've gotten great training from Steph [Buck] and Angie [Kane Ferrante]. The Purple Rose practices what it preaches: Excellence is a habit.

"Guy talks about how the universe puts you where you are meant to be," he says. "When I found the Purple Rose, I hit a gold mine."

2015 Apprentice Class with Jeff on the Annapurna set: (back row, l-r) Megan Pinto, Owen Likley, Mikey Wecht, John Forgrave; (front row, l-r) Julia Cassell, Erika Thiede, Jeff Daniels, and April Warner.

> "All the hard work builds so much grit. My interest in acting deepened and I became interested in playwriting. The greatest lessons I've learned have been life lessons: *Keep an open mind and heart.*" —MEGAN PINTO

Julia Garlotte and Wesley Speary in Dark Night performance 2007.

Megan Pinto

A Raleigh, N.C., native and Ohio Wesleyan graduate, Megan Pinto takes a welcome break from cleaning restrooms to explain that a college friend and former apprentice, April Warner, convinced her to apply for the apprenticeship. "Everything—except, possibly, the bathroom duty—has been a highlight in its own way," she says, laughing. "But I really loved the formal acting and directing workshops with Guy and Michelle." Then she quickly adds that any building expertise can be credited to her work in the shop on the sets for *Annapurna* and *Talley's Folly*.

"I've grown so much as a person and an artist. All the hard work builds so much grit. My interest in acting deepened and I became interested in playwriting. The greatest lessons I've learned have been life lessons: *Keep an open mind and heart.*"

Erika Thiede

Early one summer morning, apprentice Erika Thiede, production assistant to the stage manager, runs the 2AZ cast through a routine drill, checking the production's firearms to ensure they are safe, properly assembled, and bullet-free. Afterwards, the actors scatter and she explains, "My job as production assistant stage manager is to make sure that someone is present for every entrance and exit, to distribute and collect all props, and to give the actors whatever they need. I have a huge checklist, and it has to be very detailed. If someone is called away, someone else knows exactly what to do at all times."

A Lawrence University graduate, she worked in a college admissions office for several years before taking PRTC classes and then applying for an apprenticeship. "I would really like to create an artistic center that offers arts in collaborative ways—dance, yoga, acting—so I wanted to learn how a small non-profit is run," she says.

Dark Night Performances must utilize the set on hand. Here the class of 2008 is on the Panhandle Slim and The Oklahoma Kid *set.*

"THE PURPLE ROSE TAUGHT ME MORE IN TWO OR THREE MONTHS THAN I LEARNED IN COLLEGE AS A THEATER MAJOR. IT IS REALLY EXCITING TO WORK WITH PEOPLE WHO ARE PASSIONATE ABOUT THEIR ART." —Mikey Wecht

Her rotations began in the shop. "I'd never done anything electrical before, but in my second month, I found myself running a light board for a show. That was cool." As the year progressed, she discovered that "Every job is difficult, but in different ways."

She researched apprentice programs and asked a lot of questions before she signed on with the Purple Rose, "but this apprenticeship exceeds my expectations. Megan [Pinto] and I talk about how we're molting a lot and taking on new habits. I think it's great fun—until it's not. And then it's fun again. This job is ever-changing. There's always something new to learn."

The best parts of her apprenticeship, she says, happened when she could watch Guy during the rehearsal process, observing how a director interacts with actors. "When I studied theater in college, I learned about the academic components of the theater, but here we learn by watching and doing. I've made lifelong friends, and I've learned much more about my craft: to tell the truth on stage, focus on the other characters, and respond."

Her lessons paid off when she landed a lead role in *Casting Session* opposite Tom Whalen and David Daoust before her apprenticeship ended.

Mikey Wecht

Baltimore native Mikey Wecht is hard at work building the set of 2AZ on a hot June day when he takes a break to talk. "I love building things," he says, wiping his brow. "I love the smell of fresh-cut wood. But my real passion is directing and acting. For me, the most important part of the apprenticeship has been learning how a small professional theater runs. I had to scrap everything I learned in middle school, high school, and college."

Working with experts at the top of their fields, particularly lighting designer Noele Stollmack, was part of his reason for coming. Equally inspiring were the acting classes. "The Purple Rose taught me more in two or three months than I learned in college as a theater major. It is really exciting to work with people who are passionate about their art."

He also appreciates the bonds forged in his apprenticeship class. "I've developed management skills, grown as an actor, and learned the technical aspects of the theater—lights, sound, set design, and props," he says. "The Purple Rose is the industry standard of how professional theater should be run, particularly in the way it treats actors and directors."

THE PLAYWRITING WORKSHOP

Set designers use hammers and saws and paint to create art. Costumers use fabrics and colors. An actor's tools are words and movement. "Plays are not about what people say, but what they do," Sanville says.

On a crisp fall morning, four actors and a stage manager stand behind microphones facing a packed audience in the Chelsea District Library. As a camera rolls, they read eight plays written by students in the playwriting workshop Sanville, Mountain, and Playwright Carey Crim had offered just a week earlier.

A Marine's never-forgotten experience in Korea. A college student's dramatic confession. The loss of a life and the saving of a ship. A scientific dilemma. A betrayal. A post-divorce parting. Deathbed confessions. A tragicomic introduction to life in Alaska. The plays explore topics as diverse as the eight authors who shared three intense, hardworking, soul-baring days. Their ages range between forty-three and seventy-three, their professions vary widely, but their deep interest in playwriting is shared.

After the readings, Guy Sanville introduces the playwrights and explains the process of crafting memorable plays. "We look for revelations, not explanations," he says. "We worked to mine personal experiences for their dramatic value. These writers had only a few days to produce and polish their work. Every play is commendable."

The two-hour reading and Q&A session with the audience was one of eight the PRTC scheduled during the library's calendar year.

"This was the best thing I've done for myself in a long time," former apprentice and playwright Matt Pinard says after the applause ended.

The 2000-2001 season ended with Annie Martin's Completing Dahlia, *starring Actor/Playwright Carey Crim.*

One of the stops on the 25th Anniversary Script Preview Tour was Cleary University's Howell Campus. Chris Lutkin, Lauren Knox, Rhiannon Ragland, Tom Whalen, and Michelle Mountain helped Guy Sanville and Katie Doral give people a sneak peak of the season.

Teen Intensive

On a hot week in August, seventeen teenagers, ages thirteen to seventeen, rush to the PRTC rehearsal room early each day for the PRTC Teen Intensive. Some are local, others have come from Illinois, Ohio, and Colorado. After Michelle Mountain and Lauren Knox run through a litany of warm-up exercises, the first assignment is "Freeze Frame." The teens divide into groups, choose a fairy tale, and present it in five tableaux. "Choose the five events that best tell the story," Mountain advises. "Use your full body to tell your tale."

Once their classmates guess the story, Mountain asks, "What things tend to work better when you're trying to tell a story without words?" She demonstrates techniques with Knox.

> ## "Breathing is the cradle of emotion. If you learn to breathe—actually breathe—things will affect you in surprising, even startling, ways."
>
> —MICHELLE MOUNTAIN

Teen Intensive is fun for participants and instructors alike.

Late in the afternoon, she asks her young actors to picture the story of their monologue. "Who are you talking to? What do you need or want from them?" she asks. "No acting allowed," she adds. "We're going to teach you that the secret to acting is not to act. Stand still without acting."

"My granddaughter waited all year for this camp," one proud grandmother says. "Last year she wasn't showing any interest in grades, but I knew how much she had loved acting class, so I told her she could only attend the Teen Intensive this summer if she got her grades up. She has all A's now. That's how important this class is, at least to one girl."

Actor Boot Camp

"I spend my entire Acting I class teaching breathing and standing," Michelle Mountain tells her Boot Camp students the first morning. "Many of us have to relearn how to breathe. Our bodies can hold a gallon of air, but most of us get by with a pint, breathing very shallowly. "But, she adds, "breathing is the cradle of emotion. If you learn to breathe—actually breathe—things will affect you in surprising, even startling, ways."

THE EDUCATION

117

Tom Whalen leads movement
exercises in an acting boot camp.

The ensemble cast of Julie Johnson *mined for deep emotions in the*
winter of 1998.

Her class lies in a circle, hands at their sides, palms up, mouths open. "Now, follow the path your breath is taking into and out of your body," she suggests quietly. "When you do this, you'll become centered, alert. When you allow yourself to breathe, things start to happen, things start to affect you. Your job is to surrender to your breath, to the text, to your partner, and let all of these things affect you, and therefore, the work."

She turns off the lights, bathing the rehearsal room in shadows. "Open your eyes. Focus on one spot on the ceiling—really see that spot—and begin the first line of your monologue."

Tears pour down Susan Craves' face. Sanville kneels beside her and she confesses, "I've tapped into too many emotions. I shouldn't be here."

"Why?" he asks.

"I'm not ready," she says.

"Buck up, Buttercup," he says. "You are ready. I'm telling you, you're ready."

Months later, after being cast as Michelle Mountain's understudy in *Annapurna*, Craves says, "Guy Sanville treats each actor differently. Somehow he knows what we each need to

> "Acting is not about making up how you think someone else feels. It's about having something to draw on from deep within."
>
> —GUY SANVILLE

Matt Letscher returned to Chelsea from California to star in Lanford Wilson's Rain Dance *in 2001.*

become the very best we can be. The classes at the Purple Rose have changed me. Friends who've known me more than thirty years tell me I'm different. I always thought of myself as happy, but I never felt complete. Not until I started working on my acting skills here."

Eventually Sanville tells the class, "Stand up. Stand still. Now tell the truth." One by one, the students perform the monologues they prepared before the class. When a young man with Asperger's rushes through his lines, the director patiently works with him, word by word, over and over again. When the aspiring actor successfully delivers his lines, the class applauds enthusiastically.

"Do you want to know the best advice I ever got?" Guy Sanville asks his students at the end of the day.

They nod enthusiastically.

"Show up." He pauses, then adds, "You've been courageous enough to make a move in the direction of your dream, your goal. That's the first step. You're on your way—wherever it leads you."

Sanville ends his boot camps with a Q&A session, offering a wealth of advice collected during a forty-year career. "Acting is not about making up how you think someone else feels. It's about having something to draw on from deep within," he says. "It's the ability to express your humanity in an abstract form."

"Actors must have charisma. A sense of mission and purpose. A curiosity about people. Good listening skills."

"Don't worry about being too literal. Every work of art starts with one question: What if?"

At the end of the day, he stands and offers one last thought:

"Helen Keller said something profound: *Security is a myth. Life is a daring adventure or nothing.* Do something you're afraid of. And fail. Then, if you still want to act, God bless you." ∎

Steel Magnolias 2015

A Streetcar Named Desire 2009

Leaving Iowa 2004

"I didn't dream up the idea of the theater just to revitalize Chelsea—but I was pretty confident that when people had a reason to come to Chelsea, its businessmen and civic leaders could find a reason for them to stay and look around, maybe spend some money." --JEFF DANIELS

The Business

In its first twenty-five years, the Purple Rose staged ninety-seven productions, including fifty-five world premieres and nineteen Midwest or Michigan premieres. More than five hundred actors appeared on stage, more than 150 apprentices learned theater trades here, more than 2,500 professional and amateur actors auditioned for onstage roles, and thousands enrolled in classes. The list of the theater's awards and honors fills eight pages, single-spaced. The theater has been recognized by the American Theatre Critics Association, the National Endowment for the Arts, Actors Equity Association, the State of Michigan, the Shubert Foundation, and the Edgerton Foundation.

"We're the best theater in the state in terms of quality, and we draw people from all over the Great Lakes region," says Guy Sanville. "It took many years, the contributions of many people, and a lot of hard work to get us to this point."

CHAPTER 7
THE BUSINESS

"Jeff was a pro at putting the *fun* in *fun*draising."

—JUDY GALLAGHER

Kathleen and Jeff Daniels take a break from golfing at a Jeff Daniels Comedy Golf Jam.

> "When the Common Grill and Cleary's Pub came on the heels of the theater, it was like money in the bank for Chelsea."
>
> — ANN FEENEY

In 1990, when rumors began to circulate through Chelsea that Hollywood actor Jeff Daniels might be interested in opening a theater, Chelsea was suffering a serious economic crisis. The Health Department had closed one restaurant because of bad food. Dancer's Department Store had closed. The drug store had moved to the mall on the outskirts of town, and other downtown businesses were threatening to follow suit. Central Fibre left for Indiana. "For Sale" signs littered village streets. Old commercial buildings stood empty. Real estate prices were dropping. Walter Leonard, editor of the *Chelsea Standard*, called Chelsea "a sort of ghost town."

"We were all concerned about Chelsea's future," recalls Ann Feeney, who was working for the Chamber of Commerce at the time. "People weren't moving away, but people weren't coming here, either. Still, even in the worst of times, this has always been a really dynamic place. People here put the town first. Chelsea has always had a core of effective, problem-solving residents, and Bob Daniels was at the top of the list. His fingerprints are on everything good that happened here during his lifetime."

THE PURPLE ROSE *of* CHELSEA

As Jeff Daniels searched for theater sites, Bob Daniels went trolling for a chef interested in opening an upscale restaurant. He was successful. "Dad brought a guy named Craig Common to the theater the week of the previews for our first show," Jeff Daniels recalls. "We had been in the building just six weeks. It still needed painting. I was in the panic mode with no idea if anyone would come to see what we were trying to do. Craig asked me if I would still be here in five years. I can remember thinking, 'I've put out $300,000 of my own money, and I have absolutely no idea if this theater will fly.' I just had hope."

"Of course I will," the actor told the prospective restauranteur with a bright smile.

Common opened his restaurant in W.P. Schenk's former department store on Main Street. Within weeks, restaurant critics and theater critics had visited, sampled, and written rave reviews—of both the theater and the restaurant. Shortly afterwards, Cleary's Pub opened.

Chelsea was once again on the map.

"I didn't dream up the idea of the theater just to revitalize Chelsea—but I was pretty confident that when people had a reason to come to Chelsea, its businessmen and civic leaders could find a reason for them to stay and look around, maybe spend some money," Daniels says.

Opposite page: Sigourney Weaver read Love Letters *with Jeff at the* DIA *for a Purple Rose fundraiser after he did the same for her New York Flea Theatre.*

Below: The Pleasantville *(1998) premiere got crowds dancin' in Ann Arbor's streets.*

Plymouth Fife and Drum Corps distract our #1 golfer.

"When the Common Grill and Cleary's Pub came on the heels of the theater, it was like money in the bank for Chelsea," Ann Feeney says. "For the first time in a long time, there was optimism about the future of our community."

Fundraising for the fledgling theater was a constant concern. Daniels hired Judy Gallagher to head development efforts. "It was a challenge to work with so many creative, non-business people when I was focused on dollars and cents," she recalls. "The Purple Rose was Jeff's baby. Kathleen was the cheerleader; she attended every performance, all the fundraising events, and still made it to her kids' games. I remember Jeff coming to the theater straight from coaching T-ball for Lucas's team."

"In the early days, the studios were generous about offering us movies for fundraisers."

—JEFF DANIELS

The first PRTC Director of Development, Judy Gallagher, helped organize the comedy golf jams and movie premieres.

When Gallagher started her job, her office lacked equipment, furniture, and heat. She hijacked an apprentice to create fundraising software and began her job. She quickly learned it came with benefits. "Jeff was a pro at putting the *fun* in *fun*draising," she says. Among the highlights of her tenure were the Jeff Daniels Comedy Golf Jams and premieres of Daniels' movies.

"In the early days, the studios were generous about offering us movies for fundraisers," Daniels says. *Gettysburg* (1993) was the first PRTC premiere/fundraiser; Civil War reenactors served as ushers. *Dumb and Dumber* (1994), *Fly Away Home* (1996), *101 Dalmatians* (1996), *Pleasantville* (1998), and *Gods and Generals* (2003) followed. For the *101 Dalmatians* premiere, Jeff Daniels and several Dalmatians rode a firetruck to the Michigan Theater, where they were greeted with more Dalmatians and animal rights protesters. "We got the city of Ann Arbor to close down the street for a parade," Gallagher recalls. "Cruella was there with Dalmatians on leashes. Puppy paws were projected across the night sky."

For *Dumb and Dumber*, Daniels drove the Muttmobile. *Gods and Generals* premiered in Jackson just as the city was unveiling a new art district near the old state penitentiary. There was a double feature that night: the movie and a tour of solitary confinement cells in pitch darkness.

"We always had big VIP receptions following the premieres, and they would be packed," Gallagher says. "We held an auction afterwards, and everyone had a blast. I remember Ted Nugent telling me, 'I think you need more money for this'—a prophylactic tongue. Another year we raised $5,000 auctioning Jeff's dog's toy. We made more than $100,000 at each premiere."

The annual Jeff Daniels Comedy Golf Jams often highlighted current movies. The year *Fly Away Home* was released, the actor arrived in a vintage airplane. *Dumb and Dumber* inspired a car chase across the Polo Fields Golf Course, with Daniels' Bronco hotly pursued by a police car and "biker babes." One year a parachutist landed two feet from the actor, held out a package, and announced, "Your balls, Mr. Daniels."

"Those were great times, but they were exhausting. And a lot of work," the actor says. "Every year I wrote comedy sketches for every hole. After ten years, I was burned out." At about the same time, movie studios realized the marketing benefits of staging their own premieres, so that fundraising opportunity also ended. "That was when the board suggested I take my guitar onto the stage," Daniels says.

Everyone has fun at a golf jam when Jeff Daniels models Superbowl rings for Guy Gordon's Team.

Judy Gallagher poses with Cruella De Vil at the 101 Dalmatians *premiere in Jackson.*

The theater was on strong enough financial footing by 1999 for major construction while it closed for sixteen months. "I'm proud to say that we kept everyone on the payroll," Gallagher says. "A couple of merchants approached me, worried about the negative economic effect on the town, but together we made it through those months."

The new theater "raised the stakes here," Sanville says. "We got forty percent bigger, so we needed to sell forty percent more tickets to forty percent more people….Every decision had more weight."

In 2002, when Katie Doral apprenticed at the Purple Rose, Jeff Daniels was juggling the positions of executive director and board member with playwriting and his movie career. Eventually, he decided to take a more advisory role. "The movies had to be my top priority. I went where the work was," Daniels says. "I always kept an eye on what was happening in Chelsea, but some years brought opportunities far from home."

When he landed his first television series, *The Newsroom*, it was a "twenty-four/seven job," he says. "Those years presented us all with entirely new challenges," Sanville adds. The PRTC was experiencing major personnel changes. Judy Gallagher retired. Casey Granton

"We took a huge risk with *2AZ*. In an era when multi-million-dollar theaters are doing one-man and one-woman shows for cost reasons, we took on a play that required sixteen actors." —GUY SANVILLE

Past Apprentice Danny Brinkel does a mean Caddyshack *impersonation.*

took over as development director, and after a few years was replaced by Katie Frye Hammond. Then Managing Director Alan Ribant retired, passing the managing director responsibilities to Company Manager Julie Brunzell. When Marketing Director Heidi Bennett and Managing Director Brunzell left, the Board named William Wood temporary executive director. A month into Wood's new role, former Apprentice Katie Doral contacted Sanville, to say her family was returning to Michigan. He immediately wrote back, "There might be something here." In September, 2013, she became managing director, with a budget of almost $1.9 million.

Doral began her new job the week *The Vast Difference* opened. "No one had been in the marketing director's chair for four months, and there had been no managing director for a month, so it was a tough, very busy time. But things got much better when I hired Amy [Klain]," she says. Doral then hired another former apprentice, Lexi Cain, to help with administration, as well as Gerie Greenspan as development director.

In 2014, the PRTC budget hit $2.1 million dollars, a significant increase due largely to rises in actors' salaries and the costs of running the business, Doral says. "We're a non-profit theater. We can't pay people what they're worth, but we can offer good benefits."

"To pay the bills, the Board has learned that the theater can't just offer new plays; it needs to offer a well-known classic now and then," Board Treasurer John Mann says. "And we also know that comedy—especially Jeff's form of comedy—sells. We have to raise over $800,000 every year for our operating budget and sell over $1 million worth of tickets, so the choice of plays is critically important. That's where Guy comes in."

Despite the PRTC's strong and sustained growth, the years haven't always been copacetic. After 9/11, box office revenues dropped throughout the nation. During Michigan's Rust Belt years, starting in 2007, the theater was forced to "tighten its belt," Daniels says. In the fall of

2014, *Annapurna* closed a week early, and in the summer of 2015, the dystopian drama 2AZ closed a month early. "That had never happened before," Mann says. "Both were excellent shows, but they appealed to a narrower audience. Jeff pointed out at a board meeting that seventy-five percent of Broadway shows close within a week. That's show business. It just hadn't been our experience."

"We took a huge risk with 2AZ," Sanville says. "In an era when multi-million-dollar theaters are doing one-man and one-woman shows for cost reasons, we took on a play that required sixteen actors. The average age of our audience is fifty-four, so our key demographic didn't come because of the zombie factor, despite the fact that the zombies were peripheral to the action in the play. But a silver lining emerged from this experience. Our Board realized the thin membrane that exists between risk and failure, and they established a risk fund. Realistically speaking, we can't hit a home run every time. This fund will ensure that we stay strong financially."

"We have been very fortunate financially," Mann agrees. "We're on solid footing, thanks to the continued generosity of our donors and Board members and to the outstanding professional staff we have in place now."

Although the Board has approved plans to expand the facilities, there are no plans to expand the theater itself. "We have 168 seats and we'll stick with that—or take out the first row and go down to 154," Sanville says. "I've seen a lot of theaters fail by expanding too much. This is the right size for us, for our community. We've tapped into our share of the market. We want to keep doing what we do best. We're already stretched staff-wise."

"This is a different place, different from ninety-five percent of all theaters," he adds. "Jeff launched the theater with the understanding that we would grow and develop our own talent—and that's what we've done. Katie Doral, our Managing Director, is a former apprentice. So are Amy Klain, our Company Manager; Lexi Cain, our Office Manager; and Julia Garlotte, Box Office Manager. They understand what it takes—in all facets—to make a Purple Rose play. That's a bonus most other theaters don't have. Our people are raised in our system."

MANAGING DIRECTOR KATIE DORAL

The twenty-fifth Purple Rose season marks Katie Doral's second anniversary as managing director. "Katie and I are real partners," Sanville says. "We became a better theater the day she became managing director. We have a good budget to work with, but it's the people here who are the reason behind our success."

"We are a family," Doral agrees. "We stick with the old adage, 'Nurture our own, create our own talent.'" She is a prime example of that philosophy: she met Guy, Michelle and Jeff Daniels in an Albion College theater class, then enrolled in the Purple Rose apprenticeship program after graduation. When her apprenticeship ended, she became an assistant stage

Katie Doral.

manager and, eventually, equity stage manager. She left to fulfill a dream of working in professional children's theater, and when the managing director position opened in Chelsea, she returned home. "It was fate," she says.

In 1995, when Jeff Daniels chose Guy Sanville as artistic director, the theater's annual budget was $529,000. When Doral served her apprenticeship in 2002, the budget hit one million dollars, and the staff consisted of seven full-time employees. When she returned in 2013, the budget had doubled and the need for administrative help was greater than ever. In the theater's twenty-fifth anniversary year, Doral is ultimately responsible for managing ten full-time employees, countless part-time professionals, seven apprentices, and a $2.3 million budget.

Each forty-three-week season consists of four plays, and pre-production costs hover somewhere around $363,000 each. Actors rehearse here for 840 hours each year, during which three hundred or more performances are staged. In 2015, the average salary for a professional actor was $489 per week. "I have a lot on my plate," Doral concedes, adding, "There are exciting things on our horizon now. We're working on raising the funds for a building expansion, which would enlarge our scene shop and lobby and add our own rehearsal space, with an adjoining green room for the actors and additional office space."

COMPANY MANAGER AMY KLAIN

Amy Klain was offered a full scholarship to study engineering at Central Michigan University, but her plans changed dramatically during her freshman year, when she offered to paint sets in the theater's scene shop. On a tour of campus, her parents noticed that she took them to the theater classrooms and stage, not the engineering department. With their blessing and belt-tightening, she switched majors. Before graduating in 2000, she saw an advertisement for the Purple Rose apprenticeship program, applied, and was accepted.

"My Dad seemed more proud of me for starting the apprenticeship at the Purple Rose than any career decision he ever made," Klain says. "Every time he came to opening night here, he just glowed."

Klain was a member of the first class of apprentices to work in the newly renovated theater. "We made signs, moved furniture, set up equipment, and painted offices while we were learning the different trades. It was a very exciting time." Her apprenticeship ended with three shows because she was asked to serve as assistant stage manager for *Guys on Ice*, which earned her an equity card. "Here, stage managers do everything they can to make people feel cherished," she says.

She assisted the stage manager for six productions and managed ten. In five years she participated in 1,000 performances; the work schedule was exhausting her. "I missed my family, weddings, holidays, and birthdays," she says. "So I decided to follow another passion for a while: jewelry making." She left with the theater's thanks and a curtain call from Guy.

Company Manager Amy Hickman Klain took a break from house managing as an apprentice to pose for a picture.

Development Director Gerie Greenspan addresses Board members at the Common Grill.

> "What impressed me most was the consistently high quality of work on this stage." —JULIA GARLOTTE

For seven years, she worked in the jewelry industry and cared for her ailing father—until November 2013, when Katie Doral called and told Klain she needed a company manager. "I can't think of anyone else I'd rather have," she said. Klain accepted the job.

"I'm self-taught in finance, but I love my work," she says late one summer night after everyone else has left the offices. She is responsible for bookkeeping, payroll, bills, day-to-day accounting, gathering financial reports for grant statements, collaborating on the budget, workman's compensation, new-hire paperwork, contracts, healthcare contributions, and union negotiations for upcoming seasons.

DIRECTOR OF DEVELOPMENT GERIE GREENSPAN

When Judy Gallagher retired as director of development, she was succeeded by Casey Granton, then Katie Frye Hammond, and then Gerie Greenspan.

"One important piece of advice I can offer about managing a non-profit is the crucial importance of choosing an excellent development director," says former Board member Bill Holmes. "Between thirty and fifty percent of the theater's operating budget comes from fundraising opportunities. The Purple Rose has the dream team in place now that we have Gerie Greenspan in that position."

Greenspan came to the PRTC with fifteen years of fundraising success working with the Interlochen Center for the Arts, Ele's Place, Glacier Hills, and the University of Michigan. She led the $10 million capital campaign for the 730-seat City Opera House in Traverse City, which earned the 2006 Governor's Award in Historic Preservation.

"It's a privilege to come in here every morning," Greenspan says. "I knew I'd landed somewhere special when my first email was from Jeff himself, welcoming me. Unlike the situation with many non-profits, everyone—our donors, artists, administrators, and Board members—completely support Jeff's vision, a vision that hasn't changed in twenty-five years. The Board has established bold plans for an ambitious campaign for the sustainability of the theater, so I'll have plenty to work on in the coming months and years. It's a great challenge."

BOX OFFICE MANAGER JULIA GARLOTTE

Julia Garlotte loved theater from a very early age. She started performing in sixth grade and joined the casts of large community theaters before enrolling in the University of Michigan's Residential College in 2001. She began the PRTC apprenticeship program after her 2005 graduation.

"What impressed me most was the consistently high quality of work on this stage," she says. The highlight of her apprenticeship came during her Dark Night, for which she wrote a play based on Sanville's prompt, "Think of a time in your life when you were wronged." "It was a thrill to see it performed on stage here."

Opposite page: For the movie premier of 101 Dalmatians at the Michigan Theater, Ann Arbor closed down the street for a parade on behalf of the Purple Rose Theatre.

Below: Julia Garlotte handles a plethora of unusual requests and phone calls in her role as box office manager.

THE BUSINESS

Amy Klain works closely with Lexi Cain.

She arrived at the PRTC intending to focus on acting, but during her last rotation, she discovered sound design. "It was fun. It came easily to me, and I loved doing it," she says. Garlotte acts and designs sound for local and regional theaters on top of holding a full-time job as the PRTC box office manager. "I like the fact that the crew of apprentices is constantly changing, so I'm constantly training someone," she says. She also enjoys the interaction with theatergoers. "Lots of people have lots of things to say," she explains. "Some call us just to talk. Others want to know what Jeff Daniels is like. There are times when I feel like his publicity agent. People send plays and movie scripts to give Jeff. When *The Newsroom* aired, one person called to complain about the content and demanded to speak to Jeff. Fortunately, I was working with an apprentice named Jeff. I handed him the phone. He handled the call beautifully."

OFFICE MANAGER LEXI CAIN

Michigan State University graduate Lexi Cain served her apprenticeship in 2005, working on six shows instead of the customary four before being hired as assistant stage manager for *Escanaba in Love*. Her love for acting and directing took her to Las Vegas, where she appeared with the Second City at the Flamingo Hotel and worked for the Broadway production of *The Producers*. After Second City closed, she moved to Hollywood and spent five years acting and working for a film-based market research firm. When she decided to return to Michigan, she also returned to her Purple Rose roots.

"Katie Doral was my stage manager and mentor when I was here. She had been back just a few weeks when she told me she needed an office manager," Cain says. "It felt great to be back. I'm everyone's go-to person; my job is to do or get whatever anyone needs. This job requires long, hard hours, but I love this theater. It is constantly challenging actors and playwrights and everyone else associated with it, to do new things. Jeff Daniels is both a mentor and an inspiration to all of us."

"The Purple Rose is a huge source of community pride," says Chelsea Mayor Jason Lindauer. "It offers immeasurable cultural benefits to our citizens as well as to people throughout the region. Forty thousand people visit Chelsea every year—that's nine times our city's population. Every visitor spends, on average, between $60 and $70 here, not including theater tickets. The theater is an economic force that has a tremendous impact here—and it grows every year."

"The theater is an economic force that has a tremendous impact here—and it grows every year," says Chelsea Mayor Jason Lindauer.

Donors recognize its significant impact on the arts. The Purple Rose Gang is a new association of donors who have made a three-year, $10,000-per-year pledge. The association includes the David A. Brandon Foundation, Craig and Donna Common, Philip J. Curtis, the Feeney family, the Hamp family, Neil and Annmarie Hawkins, Richard and Leslie Helppie, the William B. Holmes family, Ron and Eileen Weiser, and Jeff and Dawn Williams. The Sage Foundation underwrites the apprentice program. The Ford Motor Company Fund, the Hamp family, and the Matilda R. Wilson Fund sponsored the twenty-fifth anniversary season. Others who have contributed more than $25,000 to the PTRC include the Herrick Foundation, Shirley J. Herrick, and the Shubert Foundation, Inc.

Local economists estimate that the Purple Rose Theatre Company has a whopping $3.6 million annual impact on Washtenaw County, while it contributes to the community in countless other ways. The PRTC offers 300-400 teaching hours each year and opportunities for acting, auditioning, directing, and playwriting.

"It's impossible to measure the effects the theater has had on our quality of life," Chamber of Commerce Director Bob Pierce says. "The Purple Rose Theatre defines today's Chelsea. It gives us our artistic groove and an important economic engine. The theater gives a big-city vibe to our small town. I cannot envision what this community would look like without the Rose." ∎

"The Purple Rose is a huge source of community pride. It offers immeasurable cultural benefits to our citizens, as well as to people throughout the region."

—JASON LINDAUER

Best of Friends 2010

Hang the Moon 1995

THE PURPLE ROSE *of* CHELSEA

Possesed 1992

PRTC
PRODUCTIONS

Two Sisters 1994

Marshall Mason told me, "You know what you should do with your life." It helps if you pick up people along the way who believe in you,… who are in your circle. When the journey gets rough and these people say, 'Stay,' you listen to them. —JEFF DANIELS

CHAPTER 8

THE CIRCLE OF FRIENDS

Jeff Daniels credits his "Circle of Friends" with helping him establish his career path; offering guidance, wisdom, and models; and supporting his dreams and aspirations. "I was lucky enough to have DiAnn L'Roy, Jim Brooks (*Terms of Endearment* director), Marshall Mason, Lanford Wilson, Woody Allen, Paul Martinez (my manager), my parents, and my wife in my circle," he says. "When the journey gets rough and these people say, 'Stay,' you listen to them. In turn, my goal is to urge others to imagine what they can be—and then reach for that."

The list of "actors" in the theater's circle of friends is long and continues to grow.

DIANN L'ROY

"DiAnn L'Roy was a one-person force who lived to put on musicals, and I was the main beneficiary," Jeff Daniels says. "Somehow, when I was in sixth grade, she saw something in me."

That year, L'Roy decided to introduce her students to the art of improvisation. She chose Jeff Daniels to play a politician giving a speech while his pants were falling down. Long beyond his allotted three minutes, he kept the class—and visitors attracted by the commotion—laughing uproariously. Later, the boy's music teacher went to his parents and insisted, "Don't let this go unnoticed."

"I remember Jeff so vividly," DiAnn L'Roy says. "I marvel at the extraordinary opportunities I had in Chelsea, in a community that recognized that the arts were important. At the time I was young, idealistic, and I didn't know I couldn't do what I wanted to do: to inspire others to love the theater."

Jeff Daniels starred on stage at an early age, in high school and community theater productions, including Oklahoma.

> "A community's emphasis—or lack of emphasis—on the arts says something important about that community. Chelsea is a place where we encourage people to think, dream, and hope." —JASON LINDAUER

When he was in sixth grade, his music teacher, DiAnn L'Roy recognized that Jeff Daniels had a flare for the dramatic.

Before coming to Chelsea, she had been a self-proclaimed "theater rat"—"never a star, but I loved everything about the theater," she says. After graduating from the University of Michigan, she landed a teaching job in Chelsea and discovered talented students she encouraged to participate in the school choir, musicals, and the thriving community theater.

"Jeff ranks as the most successful and talented, certainly, but there were many other gifted students, Kathleen [Daniels] among them," she says.

After his improvisation, she convinced Jeff Daniels to join the choir. He became one of five boys ("three of whom could sing"). By the time Daniels reached high school, half her choir consisted of boys. "Jeff had convinced the town that it was manly to sing," she explains, laughing.

For years she encouraged him to try out for school plays. "He'd sit in back of the auditorium and watch every rehearsal, but he wouldn't try out," she says. "Finally, during his sophomore year, I caught up with him leaving basketball practice, all sweaty, and told him auditions were being held for *South Pacific*. 'You will try out,' I ordered."

Daniels was cast in the chorus of sailors. "He turned a bit part into something special," L'Roy says. The following year he starred in *Guys and Dolls*. "From early on, he was a student of his craft."

During his senior year, she cast Daniels as Fagan in *Oliver*. "You don't pick *Oliver* unless you know you can cast it well," she says. "I knew by then that Jeff had the ability to do whatever he wanted to do in life." She remembers how he spent months practicing the music and discussing the character he would play.

"Give me a sense of why you're doing whatever you're doing on stage," she advised. "Build your character from the inside." Later, she realized how much he practiced at home. "From the start, he was committed to perfecting whatever he did on stage," she says.

Jeff's graduation was a bittersweet experience for his music teacher and mentor. "On the last Saturday performance, we stared at each other," she remembers. "I knew then that I'd seen something special happen before my very eyes. I've never forgotten that moment. It was a privilege."

During his middle school and high school years, Jeff Daniels juggled homework, sports, forensics team, choir, and theater.

Bob and Marjorie Daniels helped make their son's dream of the theater a reality.

She quickly adds, "I'm extraordinarily proud of Jeff's professional career, but I'm even more proud of the kind of man he is. He has done well for his family, his community, and his craft. He has given back and played forward. The Purple Rose is a testament to people believing they can do anything they want—if they all work together. And the Purple Rose is Jeff Daniels."

THE FAMILY

"The theater really is a family affair," Daphne Hodder, Jeff Daniels' mother-in-law, points out. Kathleen was Jeff's earliest supporter in his dream to launch the Purple Rose Theatre. Her sister Anne married John Mann, the banker Daniels tapped to become Board treasurer in the theater's earliest days. Jeff's parents, Bob and Marjorie Daniels, supported the theater financially and through their community involvement. The Daniels' son Lucas, a graduate apprentice, videotaped and edited the documentary *Purple Rose 25 Years*, which premiered on Detroit Public Television in October 2015. Their son Ben has performed with his father during "Jeff Daniels' Onstage & Unplugged," as well as for the theater's Annual Backyard BBQ fundraiser. Daphne Hodder provided the theater's earliest secretarial and box office services.

Jeff Daniels credits his parents with his success in life and his commitment to making his home town a vibrant center for the arts.

"I am where I am today because I always knew my parents and my wife were behind me one hundred percent," Jeff Daniels says.

Bob Daniels was also behind Chelsea one hundred percent. "In my estimation, there are four men in Chelsea who made a significant difference here," observed Chelsea lawyer John Keusch as he neared his one-hundredth birthday. At the top of his list was Bob Daniels.

"I still miss him. The whole town misses him," Ann Feeney says. "Bob worked hard for Chelsea, and he did it quietly, without any fanfare. He and Jeff are responsible for saving Chelsea from a really serious economic crisis in the late 1980s."

"The theater opening was scary for Jeff and Kathleen in the beginning," Bob Daniels told a reporter in 2001. "They were experimenting with a pretty novel idea—to turn their backs on New York and L.A., and promote Midwestern actors and playwrights. But they had a dream and they followed it. Jeff wanted to use his career to communicate with—and help—people back home. And he has. I'm proud of him."

"Bob was so smart, so kind, and in more ways than anyone will ever know he worked quietly behind the scenes to improve Chelsea. Financially and actively, he was completely behind Jeff in his commitment to making the theater work," says Daphne Hodder. "He always encouraged Jeff to do whatever he wanted to do. And Jeff's mother was just the same. Jeff is like his parents; they have such clarity of vision."

> "We are an organization where people can go to get away from their lives for two hours, to have fun, cheer, laugh and cry together."
>
> —BILL HOLMES

When she first heard Jeff's idea about starting a professional theater here in Chelsea, she thought he was crazy—"amazing, but crazy," Hodder adds, laughing. "But I'd always loved the theater, so I was all in favor of the idea. It was amazing to watch the theater go from a dream to an old garage to the cultural center it has become."

Her involvement began as a volunteer secretary for the first Board meetings. She quickly became a part-time administrator, working three days a week for six hours, with time off to watch her grandchildren's activities. "In the early days, the staff did everything by hand," she says. "I kept files, wrote the names and dates of plays on tickets, put them in white envelopes, licked them, licked the stamps, and walked down the street to mail them. At first, we didn't even take credit cards." She remembers lobbying for headphones, to help with the increasing number of phone calls. "I wouldn't have missed one minute of those years for anything," she says. "They were exciting, full of energy. I have always been impressed with the caliber of people who joined Jeff in working out his dream."

Jeff Daniels is renowned for his commitment to his family. "When Kathleen and I started our family, we returned to Chelsea because it's where we're from. It's where we had a strong family network," he says. He wrote the play A Vast Difference as a testimony to his father. "From the time my father was a little kid, his father told him, 'Make sure you leave a place better than you found it,'" Jeff Daniels says. "My father did that. And he told his kids the same thing he was told. I'm trying to pass that idea on."

THE BOARD OF DIRECTORS

"The Board has been—and continues to be—amazing," Guy Sanville says. "Co-chairs Sheila and Steve Hamp are taking the Purple Rose to a new level."

At the start of the twenty-fourth season, Dave Brandon and Bill Holmes stepped down from their places on the Board after nineteen and twenty-four years, respectively. Steven K. Hamp and Sheila Ford Hamp replaced Philip J. Curtis as co-chairs, with Peter Feeney serving as vice president, Craig Common as secretary, and John Mann as treasurer. Seated with

Based on a Native American legend, White Buffalo *was staged in 2012, with actors Nate Mitchell, Meghan Thompson, and Rainbow Dickerson.*

The 2004 PRTC Board of Directors included (standing, l-r) Richard Helppie, John Colone, Jeff Daniels, David Brandon, Ann Feeney, John Mann, Bill Holmes, and (front row, l-r) Peter Heydon, Betty Jean Awrey, Anne Colone and Craig Common.

them around the Board table are Betty Jean Awrey, John Colone, Philip J. Curtis, Ruth Roby Glancy, H. Ron Griffith, Neil Hawkins, David Larsen, Maria Leonhauser, George Moses, and Timothy L. Nasso.

Through two-and-a-half decades, the Board has included prominent members of a community that continues to grow as the theater's reputation grows. Past and honorary Board members include Founder Jeff Daniels, as well as Gail Bauer, Paul Boylan, David Brandon (past chair), Anne Colone, Jill Corr, Ann Feeney, Patric Freydl, Doug Graham, Sanjay Gupta, Richard Helppie (past chair), Peter Heydon, Bill Holmes (past chair), Atanas Ilitch, Marcia J. MacCready, Paul Martino, Michael Novak, JoAnne Rosenfeld, Judy Dow Rumelhart, Ben

Upton, Ron Weiser (past chair), Dawn Williams, and Steve Yarows. Melissa Sage Fadim, benefactor (Sage Foundation) and underwriter of the Apprentice Program, was elected Honorary Board Member.

"They are all stars!" John Mann says. "I was thrilled to be able to rub elbows with these people. We had a lot of fun together over the years."

"I had a huge learning curve. My role was business-related. I asked people to take a chance on the theater—and it worked. Failure was not an option." —BILL HOLMES

BILL HOLMES

As soon as the Garage Theatre was purchased, Jeff Daniels knocked on Bill Holmes' door at the Chelsea Milling Company, asking for help. JIFFY offered an initial check for $25,000, and Jeff offered Holmes a Board position. "I was impressed with the strength of Jeff's concept and vision, and I was sold on the proposed theater's commitment to the community," Holmes recalls. "But I told him I didn't know anything about theater."

"We'll teach you," Daniels promised.

"He did a good job over the next twenty-four years," Holmes says.

The first meeting Holmes attended was held in the basement of the old maintenance garage. Jeff Daniels laid a spare door across two sawhorses to serve as a table and the "Founding Four" (Jeff Daniels, Bartley Bauer, Doug Beaumont, and T. Newell Kring) plus Holmes and Treasurer John Mann pulled up whatever they could find for seats. "That meeting was a little more homespun than the board meetings I'd attended at St. Joseph Hospital," Holmes points out, laughing.

But it wasn't until he and his wife Wendy saw the first play that he realized the value of what the theater was offering to Chelsea and the surrounding community, he says. "My world is 180 degrees away from the artsy scene, so I had a huge learning curve. My role was business-related. I asked people to take a chance on the theater—and it worked. Failure was not an option."

He chooses one example to show how the business and creative sides of the theater work together. "The play intended for the fall of 2001 was an edgy drama, but after 9/11, Jeff and

Dennis McIntyre's play National Anthems *was staged in the spring of 1993.*

Miles & Ellie opened in June of 2013, starring Rusty Mewha and Rhiannon Ragland.

> # "My goal is always to urge people to imagine what we can be—and then reach for it."
>
> —JEFF DANIELS

Guy decided that people needed to have a reason to laugh, so they changed the play. We all scrambled to make the necessary changes. That was a good example of all of us, businesspeople and artistic people, collectively deciding what was appropriate."

By that time, the Board recognized that comedy sells tickets at a brisker pace than dramas— "But it was more than that," Holmes says. "We are an organization where people can go to get away from their lives for two hours, to have fun, cheer, laugh and cry together."

Like any business, the theater has experienced cycles: upward curves followed by plateaus, he says. "Along the way, the Board made management changes that would help us continue to provide quality theater experiences. We tried to achieve a balance, where our budget would be based on sixty percent earned revenues and forty percent fundraising."

In the summer of 2014, Holmes decided that twenty-four years was enough. "It was time to give my spot to someone else," he says. He also serves on the boards of the YMCA and St. Joseph Hospital, chairs Girls on the Run in southeast Michigan, and is past president of the University of Michigan Club of Ann Arbor, all of them time-consuming responsibilities.

"It was an honor to be asked to stay involved for so long. I'm a better, more rounded person because of the experience. I have so much respect for how hard people in the arts—both on the business and the creative sides—work."

JOHN MANN

"I'm a month older than Jeff, and we went through school together beginning in kindergarten," says Daniels' brother-in-law, John Mann, president of the Chelsea State Bank. "It was no surprise to me that Jeff became successful, but as a kid you can't predict that your friend will become a movie star."

When they were boys, they often tape recorded short stories they wrote, imitating radio shows, Mann remembers. In high school, both boys joined the forensics team—"but Jeff was head and shoulders above everyone else," the banker says. Twice the team competed on the state level. Because he was involved in both forensics and sports, Daniels surprised Mann when he tried out for a musical—"and nailed the part," his brother-in-law says. "He was a ham. He had a magnetism on the stage even then."

In 1990, when Daniels bought the old bus garage, he asked Mann, who had joined the bank staff in 1988, to become the new theater's treasurer. "From the beginning, it was fun," he says. "Everyone was so fired up about the idea of starting a theater. Jeff had the blueprint and a mission everyone could embrace. His passion and vision have always been the key to the theater's success."

THE FEENEY FAMLY

"The theater has made all the difference in the world to the success of our community," says Ann Feeney, who headed Chelsea's Chamber of Commerce during the years when Jeff Daniels was launching the Purple Rose.

The Feeneys remember watching Jeff act in high school—"and he was good," Ann said. "This community has always been blessed with great music and arts education." Years later, the couple flew to New York with the Daniels and Daphne Hodder to see Jeff perform with Christopher Reeves at the Circle Repertory Theatre in Lanford Wilson's play *Fifth of July.* "We realized that he was an extraordinary actor who never disappoints."

The family has been enthusiastic Purple Rose supporters from its earliest days. Shortly after watching *Kuru,* the first play in the 1991/2 season, Ann and Mike Feeney wrote a check for $500 to sponsor a chair in the new theater. As owners of Arco, they also support the theater corporately. Avid golfers, they attended the Jeff Daniels Comedy Golf Jams for years, and Ann served on the Board from 2003 through 2009.

"FROM THE BEGINNING, IT WAS FUN. EVERYONE WAS SO FIRED UP ABOUT THE IDEA OF STARTING A THEATER. JEFF HAD THE BLUEPRINT AND A MISSION EVERYONE COULD EMBRACE. HIS PASSION AND VISION HAVE ALWAYS BEEN THE KEY TO THE THEATER'S SUCCESS."

—John Mann

> **"I think fame is the most overvalued thing, but it can be applied to great uses. I appreciate and respect Jeff's contributions to the community."** —PETER FEENEY

Michael Brian Ogden (l) wrote and starred in Corktown *in 2011.*

"Finances were a challenge then. Those were rough years for Michigan's economy. But the Board raised $500,000 to support the theater, and each year the budget kept getting bigger and the theater kept producing great plays," she says.

Supporting the theater has become a family affair. When Ann Feeney left the Board, her son Peter joined it. A high school classmate of Kathleen Daniels, he had played basketball and softball with Jeff Daniels when they were youngsters. Now he lives in the house where Jeff grew up.

"I didn't have to think about it when I was asked to join the Board. I said yes right away," Peter Feeney recalls. "My involvement with the theater evolved over time. I was impressed with the idea of something world-class being located in our little town. From the get-go, the theater has been an important part of Chelsea. Now, its sphere of influence is spreading; it's increasingly more important to Southeast Michigan."

When Peter Feeney took his mother's place on the Board, Michigan's economy was still a major concern. He watched Jeff Daniels make tough decisions about the staffing and the theater's future. "We regrouped and assembled a really good core of people. Now we have a strong administration—Guy, Michelle Mountain, Katie Doral, Gerie Greenspan, and others—who do the hard work behind the scenes."

He adds, "I think fame is the most overvalued thing, but it can be applied to great uses. I appreciate and respect Jeff's contributions to the community. For that reason, the Purple Rose ranks really high in our family's benevolences. When we decide where to contribute, we look at the product and at the community. We make contributions based on faith and how people contribute to the world. Contributing to the Purple Rose makes Chelsea a better place and strengthens the arts immeasurably. When my siblings and I travel, we tell people we're from Chelsea, Michigan, and often we find that people in faraway places know about our theater."

CRAIG COMMON

"The downtown was nearly dead, and we faced a major decision," Bob Daniels told a reporter in 2001, looking back at what was probably the most significant crossroads in Chelsea's history. "We could let it die. Or we could figure out new uses for the downtown." In 1990, he began casting feelers to entrepreneurs who might be interested in taking a chance on Chelsea. One well-known Ann Arbor restaurant manager told Daniels, "Chelsea is too small." But a day or so later, he walked past the table where Bob and Marjorie Daniels were dining and placed a business card on the table. "Craig Common" and his phone number were written on the card.

Within days, Daniels and several other Chelsea businessmen introduced Common to Chelsea. Common was hooked, but his financial backer was not.

"Give me twenty-four hours," Daniels said.

He called six people he thought would be interested in jointly offering $30,000 to finance a new, upscale restaurant in town. They all said yes. "Bob Daniels was the wisest and most

Craig Common (far right) sponsored golf teams with friends during the years of the Jeff Daniels Comedy Golf Jams.

honest guy I've ever met, so I knew he wouldn't steer me wrong," Craig Common says. "At the time, Chelsea had a bunch of empty buildings, no nice signs, no parking lot behind the building. But Bob Daniels gathered his "posse" of local business people with a vision for the downtown. By Thanksgiving 1990, I decided to go for it."

According to Dave Brandon, "The Common Grill has an enormous impact on the theater—and vice-versa. It offers theatergoers a special night out on the town: dinner and theater. The Common Grill gave the theater a place where we could host events and meet with donors. I'd say the Common Grill was the best thing that could have happened to the Purple Rose."

""Those early days were such fun," Common says. "I had a terrific mentor in Bob Daniels. Jeff and I were both young and excited about our careers. And, like the theater, we've stayed true to ourselves and what we do best. Jeff and I have both had a long and very satisfying run. I'm proud of what the theater has accomplished, and I'm proud of my family's association with the Daniels family."

Above:
Carey Crim and Wayne David
Parker starred in Lanford Wilson's
Book of Days in 1998.

Opposite page:
Jeff Daniels launched the Purple Rose
Theatre to promote a love of the arts
for people of all ages.

DAVE BRANDON

"I've been exposed to some outstanding business minds, but Dave Brandon has the sharpest of any I know," says John Mann.

Several years after the Purple Rose opened, Dave Brandon met Jeff Daniels when they were paired in a charity celebrity golf tournament sponsored by Bo Schembechler. "It was a long, long event," Brandon says. "We spent five hours together. During the course of the day, he asked me if my family was interested in the arts. 'We're interested in all kinds of things,' I told him. And that was the beginning of my relationship with the Purple Rose."

Brandon, who had loved performing during his high school and college years, joined the board of directors in 1996.

"So much happened during that time," says the former CEO of Valassis Communications (eleven years) and Domino's (eleven years). "We renovated the theater, revamped the lobby, expanded the administrative offices, and experimented with a lot of things, some successful, some not. We were always trying to strike a balance between artistic expression and paying the bills. But we always stayed true to the mission of the theater." One of his personal highlights, he says, was the Burn-the-Mortgage party he hosted at his home.

"The Purple Rose was a small entrepreneurial place," Brandon says. "When I first came, the Board consisted of eight or nine people sitting in a back room on folding chairs and cardboard boxes, trying to figure out how to keep the theater alive. We discussed everything from buying the land next door to ticket prices, how much to depend on fund-raising and capital campaigns, how much to spend on facilities. At one time we thought about expanding the theater even further, but we shied away from making that commitment. And that was a good thing, in my opinion. But always the one constant in every decision was to respect and nurture the mission of the theater, to provide opportunities for talent and to provide a quality theater experience in Chelsea."

He says he is proud of the fact that during his tenure the Board put the theater on solid financial footing. "We lived through some pretty tough times: 9/11 and the 2007/2008 financial crisis in particular," he notes. "I'm proud that I was able to leave at the other end of the spectrum: with a very strong balance sheet; a well-maintained building; a strong professional administrative staff; and a highly talented group of performers, technical experts, and apprentices."

RICHARD HELPPIE

"I was a typical blue-collar kid without any role model for success, but I knew when I was little that I would run businesses." Richard Helppie says. "At thirteen, I began working with computers. At eighteen, I started my own company. I had some college classes, but for the most part, I learned by doing."

Board chairman and CEO of Santa Rosa Holdings and founder and managing partner of Vineyard Capital Group, Helppie's career focus has been broadly based: business services, IT ("forty-one years"), and healthcare ("thirty-four years"). He is credited with revolutionizing the healthcare information technologies by advocating a mobile workforce, national deployment, and significantly reduced overhead. "At one stage, I tried retirement, but flunked," he says. So he started a real estate company with his son, and he founded the Helppie Family Charitable Foundation with his wife Leslie.

Many of the Helppies' philanthropies focus on education and children's healthcare, but one day, a "friend of a friend" mentioned that the Purple Rose Theatre needed strong businesspeople to help establish its financial base. The Helppies met with Jeff Daniels and Guy Sanville to learn more.

"I'm not a person who chases movie stars, so I actually had no idea how big a deal Jeff Daniels was. The only movie I'd seen him in was *Gettysburg*," Helppie says. "What attracted me to the theater was Jeff Daniels' entrepreneurism. I realized this guy was an entrepreneur trying to do something in a small Michigan town that he could do in L.A. or Chicago. I told them, 'I can't sing, dance, or act, but I know how to organize things in the business world.'"

Daniels asked him for a one-year commitment to serve on the Board. Eight times. The Helppies joined Jeff Daniels and Guy Sanville in New York for a performance of *Rain Dance* and a chance to hear how the professionals judge performances. "Fascinating," he says.

Richard Helppie retired from the PRTC Board in 2011, but continues to be a strong supporter. "The Purple Rose is a real gem. I brought boatloads of people here. My one regret is that I wasn't successful at convincing metro Detroit about how accessible Chelsea is. My involvement rounded our lives and perspectives. I still can't sing, dance, or act, but I am a terrific audience member."

PHILIP J. CURTIS

"As a member of the Board for fourteen years, I've seen firsthand the challenges and dedication necessary to operate a world-class theatre," says Philip J. Curtis, an attorney with Curtis, Curtis & Brelinski in Jackson. "I have a deep appreciation for the work required to produce outstanding plays time and time again. The Board is continually exploring the best ways to support the artistic mission at the heart of the theater."

The actors make their work look so effortless that audience members might take their craft for granted, he adds. "My wife Kim and I have a deep appreciation for what goes into every play—including the financial aspects." A founding member of the Purple Rose Gang, a frequent sponsor of plays, and the husband of the executive director of the Jackson School for the Arts, he adds, "We are proud to support the production of new and classic American plays, as well as the perpetuation of a creative home for both emerging and seasoned artists. When we sit in the audience, we are always transported into a different world. Time seems to stop. We leave the theater either crying or laughing or both, because we are so moved. The plays stay with us long after the standing ovation. Our lives are better for the experience."

"WE LIVED THROUGH SOME PRETTY TOUGH TIMES: 9/11 AND THE 2007/2008 FINANCIAL CRISIS IN PARTICULAR. I'M PROUD THAT I WAS ABLE TO LEAVE AT THE OTHER END OF THE SPECTRUM." —Dave Brandon

> "The great thing about the Purple Rose is that anyone can become involved here if they have the energy and interest." —STEVEN HAMP

> "All of us on the Board know we can make a difference—and we have fun doing it."
>
> —SHEILA FORD HAMP

STEVEN K. & SHEILA FORD HAMP

Jeff Daniels visited Steve and Sheila Ford Hamp at their Ann Arbor home to introduce them to the Purple Rose Theatre and its mission. "We're the parents of three boys who grew up with *Dumb and Dumber*," Sheila says. "The first time we met Jeff, he was everything we all hoped he would be: funny, relaxed, friendly, and utterly committed to the mission of his theater."

Until that time, much of the Hamps' personal and professional activities centered on Detroit and Dearborn, Steve Hamp says. "But at this stage, we're interested in getting more involved in our own community. Unlike larger organizations that are totally closed, the great thing about the Purple Rose is that anyone can become involved here if they have the energy and interest."

"And, of any organization I've been engaged with, it's the most fun," Sheila adds. "All of us on the Board know we can make a difference—and we have fun doing it."

The Hamps joined the Board during the PRTC's twentieth anniversary year. Five years later, they agreed to serve as co-chairs. "I describe the Purple Rose as artisanal, home-crafted, hand-crafted, venerable, and valuable," Steven Hamp says. "High-quality, intimate, excellent, and blessed with a significant level of talent," his wife adds.

A principal with Hamp Advisors, Steven Hamp was named vice president and chief of staff at the Ford Motor Company after twenty-seven years at The Henry Ford. He also serves as chairman and president of the Michigan Educational Excellence Foundation and chairman of the Cultural Alliance for Southeast Michigan and the Henry Ford Learning Institute. In 1999, the *Detroit News* named Hamp Michiganian of the Year. In 2000, he received the first Helen and William Milliken Distinguished Service Award from the Michigan Environmental Council.

Sheila is the great-granddaughter of Henry Ford, the daughter of William Clay Ford Sr., and a member of Yale's first class of women graduates. An avid Lions fan (and vice chair of the franchise), her philanthropic interests include the Henry Ford Museum, where she is vice chairman of the Board; the Henry Ford Hospital; the Ford Motor Company Fund; and the College for Creative Studies. "We think carefully before we take on any more responsibilities, but we believe in the Purple Rose and its mission," she says. "This is an exceptionally high-quality theater with deep core values."

"The theater's visibility, strength, productions, audience, and operating funds are all things the Board is focusing on," Steve Hamp says. "But we need reserve funds. Our goal is sustainability, to get an actual risk fund and endowment established."

"We also need to reach out to the millennial generation," his wife adds. "That doesn't mean that we have to change the productions, but we need to institute ways of communication that are authentic and relevant."

When the Hamps joined the Board, Jeff Daniels' career was taking him farther from home; he had accepted a role on *The Newsroom* and temporarily moved to California. "The deep underlying question was how the theater would survive without his day-to-day involvement," Sheila says. "It was a terrific exercise for the Board, to get the place to stand on its own two feet with whatever time and effort Jeff Daniels could offer. We learned that the organization could survive. Now he's back, and we're reaching a new level of success."

COMMUNITY SUPPORTERS

MAYOR JASON LINDAUER

"There is absolutely no downside to having a theater of this quality in town," Chelsea Mayor Jason Lindauer says. "At any one time, the theater employs seventy-seven people and develops homegrown talent, preparing them for careers in theater. It has a significant financial impact on our community. It also enriches the lives of those of us who live within its radius. A community's emphasis—or lack of emphasis—on the arts says something important about that community. Chelsea is a place where we encourage people to think, dream, and hope."

Among those who come to think, dream, and hope are volunteers, who contribute an average of 2,762 hours to the theater each year.

Founder Jeff Daniels turned a dream into a reality.

Opposite page: Steve and Sheila Ford Hamp became Board co-chairs in 2015, when Guy Sanville celebrated his twentieth year as artistic director.

"ONE THING THAT IS MADE PERFECTLY CLEAR TO VOLUNTEERS HERE AT THE ROSE IS THAT WE ARE APPRECIATED. VOLUNTEERS BECOME PART OF THE PURPLE ROSE FAMILY." —George Till

JEREMY MONTANGE

On a summer day in 2015, Jeremy Montange drives to Novi with a carload of actors to publicize 2AZ at the Comic-Con convention. His involvement with the theater dates back to 1993, and earlier. A long-time Chelsea resident, he remembers riding his bicycle to the original building when it was a pizza joint. These days, he volunteers as an usher, fundraising volunteer, and jack-of-all-trades. He engraved a silver cigarette case for *Bus Stop*; found twenty copies of books with purple covers for *The Late Great Henry Boyle*; repaired jewelry, loaned a watch chain, and tracked down a bird trap for *The Stone Carver*; donated the "blood" bags for several plays; loaned a dream catcher, drum, and lasso for *White Buffalo*; and scouted canine talent for *The Last Romance*, serving as dog wrangler.

"I've attended every opening night since 1993, and I'm still amazed at the way a play comes together with the efforts of so many talented people," he says. "The theater is my social, volunteer, and philanthropic outlet. I've made amazing friends here. I've seen transformative plays here. I cannot imagine what Chelsea would be like without the Purple Rose."

JIM MYLES

"The Purple Rose and Chelsea Milling Company are the two powerhouses bringing visitors to Chelsea, but our business is directly related to, and affected by, the theater. I would attribute sixty percent of our revenue to the Purple Rose," says Jim Myles, a member of the city council and owner of the Chelsea House, which is separated from the theater by a parking lot.

"We wouldn't be in business without the theater crowd."

Out-of-town guests often dine at the Common Grill, watch theater productions at the Purple Rose, and sleep at the Chelsea House. So do guest artists and playwrights like Carey Crim. Myles offers artists and performers cut rates and the chance to stay within an easy walk of the theater. "Kim and I have had our lives enriched by the people we watch on stage and the folks working behind the scenes," he says.

GEORGE TILL

On a hot day in the summer of 2015, George Till receives an SOS from Properties Manager Danna Segrest, asking to borrow several antiques. When he delivers them, he pauses in the lobby to chat. "I really enjoy helping out at the theater," Till says. "It's a place with high energy and great, great people."

Till himself has a passing acquaintance with acting: he is a Civil War reenactor who has been an extra in Civil War-era films and documentaries.

George Till and his wife Dianne bought their Civil War-era home near the theater in 1985. They immediately became involved with the community, particularly the Chelsea Area Historical Society and Greenfield Village. Soon after the 2001 reopening of the Purple Rose, Judy Gallagher asked Till if he could volunteer as a tour guide, in Civil War uniform, for a fundraiser at the Michigan Theatre celebrating the release of Jeff Daniels' film *Gods and Generals*. He agreed. He had been hooked by the fun and the value the theater offers the community during the release of Jeff Daniels' film *Gettysburg*.

"I knew Bob Daniels well, and I admired him tremendously," Till says. "He told me once, 'When you get off Old U.S. 12, the air is different. You need to volunteer in the community, George, because you can help make Chelsea a better, more welcoming place'." Till listened. He volunteers countless hours with the theater, ushering, distributing posters, helping with mailings, working on fundraisers, lending props, offering theater tours, and even manning a paint brush now and then.

"Non-profits never have as much money as they need," he says. "There is a lot of satisfaction in becoming involved in the community and lending a hand when help is needed. One thing that is made perfectly clear to volunteers here at the Rose is that we are appreciated. Volunteers become part of the Purple Rose family."

The Civil War reenactor is no stranger to ghosts; on at least two occasions late at night on battlefields, he has come face-to-face with figures he believes are fallen soldiers. "General Joshua Chamberlain once wrote, 'Souls linger on battlefields'," Till says, adding, "I think that's true of the theater as well. I believe memorable characters from great plays can linger in a theater's atmosphere. People might think I'm loony, but I became involved in reenacting because I thought soldiers might speak through me. And that's how actors work: through their words and actions, characters come alive and speak through them. It's exciting to see that happen." ∎

"General Joshua Chamberlain once wrote, 'Souls linger on battlefields.' I think that's true of the theater as well."

—GEORGE TILL

THE FUTURE
Jeff Daniels

"**I had a dream** to make new American plays—written by Michigan folks—available to theatergoers. I wanted to give Michigan's twenty-one-year-olds a chance to act in plays directed by local directors, on sets designed and lit by local experts. We've done that here at the Rose—and I'm proud of what we've accomplished.

I want the Purple Rose to outlast me, to outlast Guy. I want live theater to continue to have a place at the table many, many years from now.

I passed on the things I learned at the Circle Rep to Guy and Michelle, and in turn they have passed them on to generations of apprentices and actors. I would love to think that in one hundred years, I'd still be able to come here, enjoy a play, and see the same commitment to quality theater."

THE PURPLE ROSE THEATER COMPANY PRODUCTIONS

1991

*Blush at Nothing***
by Lisa A. Wing
February 7-March 24, 1991

*Shoe Man***
by Jeff Daniels
April 25-July 21, 1991

1991/1992

Kuru
by Josh C. Manheimer
September 5-October 27, 1991

*Ties That Bind***
by Kitty Dubin
Nov 14, 1991-January 5, 1992

More Fun Than Bowling
by Steven Dietz
January 23-April 12, 1992

*The Tropical Pickle***
by Jeff Daniels
May 7-August 30, 1992

1992 / 1993

Possessed: The Dracula Musical
Book by Robert Marasco
& Jason Darrow
Music by Carter Cathcart
October 1-December 20, 1992

Necessities
by Velina Hasu Houston
January 14-March 7, 1993

National Anthems
by Dennis McIntyre
April 1-June 5, 1993

*Nooner***
by Kim Carney
June 17-August 29, 1993

1993/1994

*The Vast Difference***
by Jeff Daniels
October 7, 1993-January 9, 1994

*Two Sisters***
by T. E. Williams
January 27-March 20, 1994

Keely and Du
by Jane Martin
March 31-May 22, 1994

Stanton's Garage
by Joan Ackermann
June 9-August 28, 1994

1994/1995

*Thy Kingdom's Coming***
by Jeff Daniels
October 6-December 23, 1994

*Only Me and You***
by Kim Carney
January 19-March 12, 1995

*Hang the Moon***
by Suzanne Burr
March 31-May 21, 1995

Weekend Comedy
by Jeanne and Sam Bobrick
June 8-August 20, 1995

1995/1996

*Escanaba in da Moonlight***
by Jeff Daniels
September 28-December 23, 1995

Beast on the Moon
by Richard Kalinoski
January 18-March 10, 1996

The Purple Rose
Spring Comedy Festival***
by various playwrights
March 28-May 19, 1996

*The Harmony Codes***
by Michael Grady
June 6-August 25, 1996

1996/1997

*Apartment 3A***
by Jeff Daniels
September 26-December 21, 1996

*Labor Day***
by Kim Carney
January 16-March 8, 1997

The Hot L Baltimore
by Lanford Wilson
March 27-May 31, 1997

Off the Map
by Joan Ackermann
June 19-August 23, 1997

1997/1998

Escanaba in da Moonlight
by Jeff Daniels
September 18-December 20, 1997

Julie Johnson
by Wendy Hammond
January 22-March 14, 1998

*Book of Days***
by Lanford Wilson
April 2-June 27, 1998

*Marcus is Walking***
by Joan Ackermann
July 16-September 12, 1998

1998/1999

*Boom Town***
by Jeff Daniels
October 8-December 19, 1998

*The Hole***
by Wendy Hammond
January 28-March 20, 1999

The Big Slam
by Bill Corbett
April 8-June 12, 1999

Criminal Genius
by George F. Walker
July 1-August 22, 1999

1999/2000

The PRTC moved into temporary offices
in September 1999 while the building
underwent a 16-month renovation project.

2000/2001

*Rain Dance***
by Lanford Wilson
January 11-March 17, 2001

*Orphan Train: An American Melodrama***
by Dennis North
April 12-June 16, 2001

*Completing Dahlia***
by Annie Martin
July 12-September 1, 2001

2001/2002

Guys on Ice
by James Kaplan & Fred Alley
October 4-December 22, 2001

*Months on End***
by Craig Pospisil
January 17-March 16, 2002

Born Yesterday
by Garson Kanin
April 4-June 15, 2002

*Let It Be***
by Dennis North
July 11-August 31, 2002

2002/2003

*Across the Way***
by Jeff Daniels
September 26-December 21, 2002

*Stand***
by Toni Press-Coffman
January 23-March 15, 2003

*Hope for Corky***
by Randall Godwin
April 3-May 31, 2003

Blithe Spirit
by Noel Coward
June 19-August 30, 2003

2003/2004

The Good Doctor
by Neil Simon
October 2-December 20, 2003

*Leaving Iowa***
by Tim Clue & Spike Manton January
22-March 13, 2004

The Underpants
by Carl Sternheim, Adaptation
by Steve Martin
April 1-June 5, 2004

*Duck Hunter Shoots Angel***
by Mitch Albom
June 24-September 18, 2004

2004/2005

The Mystery of Irma Vep
by Charles Ludlam
October 7-December 18, 2004

*Norma & Wanda**
by Jeff Daniels
January 20-March 19, 2005

Bus Stop
by William Inge
April 7-June 4, 2005

*And the Winner Is**
by Mitch Albom
June 23-September 24, 2005

2005/2006
The Glass Menagerie
by Tennessee Williams
October 20-December 17, 2005

*Guest Artist**
by Jeff Daniels
January 19-March 18, 2006

The Late Great Henry Boyle
by David MacGregor
April 6-June 3, 2006

Honus and Me
by Steven Dietz
based on the novel by Dan Gutman June
22-September 2, 2006

2006/2007
*Escanaba In Love**
by Jeff Daniels
Sept 28, 2006-January 20, 2007

The Subject Was Roses
by Frank D. Gilroy
February 8-March 17, 2007

*When the Lights Come On**
by Brian Letscher
April 5-June 2, 2007

*Sea of Fools**
by Matt Letscher
June 21-September 1, 2007

2007/2008
*The Poetry of Pizza**
by Deborah Breevort
October 4-December 22, 2007

*Vino Veritas**
by David MacGregor
January 17-March 8, 2008

*Growing Pretty**
by Carey Crim
March 27-April 23, 2008

*Panhandle Slim & The Oklahoma Kid**
by Jeff Daniels
June 19-September 27, 2008

2008/2009
Apartment 3A
by Jeff Daniels
October 16-December 20, 2008

A Streetcar Named Desire
by Tennessee Williams
January 22-March 21, 2009

*Bleeding Red**
by Michael Brian Ogden
April 9-May 30, 2009

*Wake**
by Carey Crim
June 18-August 22, 2009

2009/2010
*Escanaba**
by Jeff Daniels
Sept 17, 2009 - January 23, 2010

*Gravity**
by David MacGregor
February 11-March 27, 2010

Our Town
by Thornton Wilder
April 15-May 29, 2010

Boeing-Boeing
by Marc Camoletti
adapted by Beverley Cross
June 17-September 11, 2010

2010/2011
*Best of Friends**
by Jeff Daniels
October 14-December 18, 2010

*Corktown**
by Michael Brian Ogden
January 20-March 5, 2011

*Some Couples May...**
by Carey Crim
March 24-May 28, 2011

*Consider the Oyster**
by David MacGregor
June 16-September 3, 2011

2011/2012
Escanaba in da Moonlight
by Jeff Daniels
September 22 - December 31, 2011

A Stone Carver
by William Mastrosimone
January 19 - March 10, 2012

*White Buffalo**
by Don Zolidis
March 29 - June 2, 2012

On Golden Pond
by Ernest Thompson
June 21 - September 1, 2012

2012/2013
Superior Donuts
by Tracy Letts
September 20 - December 15, 2012

*The Meaning of Almost Everything**
by Jeff Daniels
January 10 - March 9, 2013

33 Variations
by Moisés Kaufman
March 28 - June 1, 2013

*Miles & Ellie**
by Don Zolidis
June 20 - August 31, 2013

2013/2014
The Vast Difference
by Jeff Daniels
September 19 - December 18, 2013

Redwood Curtain
by Lanford Wilson
January 16 - March 15, 2014

*The PRTC Spring Comedy Festival:
Lovers, Liars & Lunatics**
by various playwrights
April 3 - May 24, 2014

The Last Romance
by Joe DiPietro
June 12 - August 30, 2014

2014/2015
Annapurna
by Sharr White
September 18 - December 13, 2014

Steel Magnolias
by Robert Harling
January 15 - March 14, 2015

Talley's Folly
by Lanford Wilson
April 2 - May 23, 2015

*2AZ**
by Michael Brian Ogden
June 11 - July 26, 2015

2015/2016 (25th Anniversary)
*Casting Session**
by Jeff Daniels
September 17 - December 19, 2015

The Odd Couple
by Neil Simon
January 21 - March 26, 2016

*Gaps in the Fossil Record**
by Matt Letscher
April 14 - May 28, 2016

Morning's At Seven
by Paul Osborn
June 16 - September 3, 2016

*World Premiere

ABOUT THE AUTHOR...

CYNTHIA FURLONG REYNOLDS

THIS BOOK was a labor of love for the author. To work with such talented, creative, gifted, and generous artists and administrators for months on end is a dream come true for any writer.

At a very early age, author/journalist/educator Cynthia Furlong Reynolds realized that her calling was helping people tell their stories—and she reveals how that happened in a picture book that won a 2008 Mom's Choice Award: *Grammie's Secret Cupboard*. She has written a dozen children's books, several novels, numerous personal life stories, a writing manual and workbook, and nine histories, two of which won Michigan Notable Book Awards: *Our Hometown: America's History as Seen through the Eyes of a Midwestern Village* and *JIFFY: A Family Tradition*. Currently, she is completing another Chelsea history, *A Village at War*, and a YA novel based on the World War I experiences of Chelsea native Albert Lindauer.

Her career began as a journalist; she worked for the *Portland Times, St. Petersburg Times*, and *Omaha World Herald*, as well as for Princeton University, the University of Tampa, and Creighton University. Her byline has appeared in dozens of magazines, journals, and newspapers around the country.

A graduate of the College of William & Mary and the Stonecoast Master in Fine Arts degree program (Creative Writing), she frequently works in schools as an author-in-residence, teaches writing in college classrooms and workshops, and volunteers with the Michigan Council for the Humanities in its Prime Time literacy program for at-risk families.

Her work has received awards from the Michigan Librarians' Association, the Indiana Librarians' Association, University Network Publishing, Council for the Advancement and Support of Education, Good Housekeeping magazine, and the Tampa Advertising Club.

Reynolds considers the most memorable quotes from **The Purple Rose of Chelsea** are rooted in the experiences of Jeff Daniels (*You know what you should do….Make a place better before you leave it.*) and Guy Sanville (*Fire the judge…Security is a myth. Life is a daring adventure or nothing. Do something you're afraid of. And fail. Then, if you still want to act/write/ etc., God bless you.*)

www.CynthiaFurlongReynolds.org

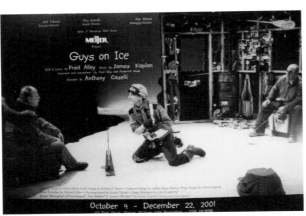

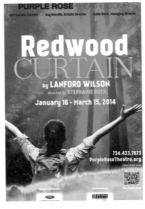